Nothing bu
from cotton fields to colonel

A story of survival, recovery, hope, victory, and resilience
by

Paula F. Penson
Colonel (Retired), USAF

*All net proceeds are donated to the Alex Francies college scholarship
fund for military members and dependents.*

Dedications

This book is dedicated to the people who have loved me, sometimes in spite of myself.

First, to David S. Penson, my husband of 20 years, who calmed me and convinced me I was worthy of unconditional love.

To my children, Chrystie, Alex, and Cynthia, without whom I am nothing.

To Sara, Trinity, and Baby Shawhan, my grandchildren, who have taught me the purity of love given with no expectation than to be loved.

To my stepchildren, Dave Jr. and Jenny, who allow me to love them as my own.

To my Houser grandchildren, Alexandra, Amy, and Ashley, who have been mine to cherish and spoil for almost 20 years.

To the extended Penson families who adopted me and brought me into their fold with unqualified acceptance: the Drakes, the Williams, the Hills, and the Hancocks.

Finally, I have to acknowledge my mother, Alene Gragg. She was poor all her life, but she never allowed us to be "dirt" poor. She figured out that education was the only guaranteed road out of poverty. For that alone, I owe her everything I have accomplished in my professional life. She taught me to be strong and to never give up. She taught me resilience and gave me hope of a better life.

THE SUCKER PUNCHES OF MY LIFE

The following significant emotional events are

the sucker punches of my life.

- Raised in poverty, migrant workers
- Teenage pregnancy at 17
- Gave up child for adoption at 18
- Father shot and killed mother at age 18
- Attempted suicide at 22
- Divorced three times by the age of 35
- Fired three times by the age of 35
- Killed a person in car accident at age 40
- Son died at the age of 17, when I was 42
- Diagnosed with cancer at age 47

This book is not a "woe-is-me" book. It is the story of survival, recovery, hope, and victory. It is the story of a lifetime of resilience. It is my sincere hope that sharing this story will give others hope and victory over their own sucker punches of life.

Table of Contents

Chapter 1

I didn't know we were poor

I rode to the cotton fields in the back of an open pickup truck. My parents, sisters, aunts, uncles and cousins all piled out. Mom and Dad slung long, slender linen bags onto the left side of their bodies to hold the cotton, and canvas bladders of water on their right. Large hats shielded their faces from the Arizona summer sun.

My parents would start at the beginning of a row of cotton, picking as quickly as they could, stuffing the fluffy white cotton bolls into the linen bags. My sisters and I would follow behind, using our smaller hands to pick where the cotton was harder to reach.

Fifty years later I realize how strenuous and back-breaking the work must have been for my parents. They got thirty-five cents for each pound of cotton we picked. Thirty-five cents. I can't even imagine what that worked out to be an hour. Pennies.

But for the children, working in the fields was fun! We threw cotton bolls at each other, giggling and running up and down the rows. It was glorious to be outside, with our time in the fields broken up by breaks and lunch, where we would eat bologna sandwiches in the shade of the parked pickup trucks. At two in the afternoon, we were done, and we went home to our little one-bedroom house, where my parents did home chores under the swamp cooler. We played outside until suppertime. Our favorite game was hide-n-seek. There was no television or radio.

Some summers we would travel to Eugene, Oregon, to pick string beans, strawberries, and cherries. I remember those road trips vividly. It was an adventure. In the days before car seats and even seat belts, I always rode and slept in the back window of our little sedan because I was the smallest. I would face out the back window and watch the scenery and other cars. It was an amazing way to travel. I love long road trips to this day.

Our little town, El Mirage, was filled with migrant workers, three-quarters of whom were Hispanic. The rest were about equal numbers of African Americans and poor white people. We used an outhouse until I was nine years old. This was just how we lived.

I had no idea that other people lived differently. We accepted our situation as normal. I had just two dresses, one to wash and one to wear. I got a new pair of shoes at the beginning of each school year, and I know my mother hoped and prayed they would last until the end of the school year. If we outgrew our shoes during the year, my mother cried—she just didn't have the money to buy us another pair of new shoes. We went to the second-hand store to get a used pair to get us through the school year. We had hand-me-downs as play clothes; jeans for children did not exist. We got a pair of fifteen-cent rubber flip-flops to wear during the summer instead of our school saddle-shoes.

I was surrounded by family. My father had three brothers and four sisters. I had hundreds of cousins; two of my aunts had 13 children each. Everyone was poor. I didn't know I was poor because everyone was the same.

My mother was fanatical about cleanliness; we had baths every day and washed our hair once a week. "Just because we're poor," my mother would say, "doesn't mean we have to be dirty." We never had runny, snotty noses or dirty faces. She constantly made us wash up, blow our noses, and brush our teeth. I did not realize just how important this approach to our health was then. She did what she could within her control to give us the best life she could give us... up to and including clean faces, teeth, and hands. In retrospect, I realized we were rarely sick. It's a good thing; she sure couldn't afford a doctor bill for five kids. I was the laundress for the seven of us. Every weekend I did the laundry. My dad taught me to iron, and to this day, even if something is labeled wash-and-wear, I still want to iron it.

My mother was my greatest supporter and cheerleader. When I was in second grade, Mom and I were called to the principal's office. Evidently, I had been tested and achieved a very high score. I remember well his solemn words to my mother: "If Paula is given the right encouragement and support, she could go to college." College! What a magical word to my mom. It became her life's dream to see me go to college.

My dad had a sixth grade education and was functionally illiterate. At the end of her eighth grade year, my grandmother refused to allow Mom to attend high school. My grandfather was an alcoholic (both my grandfathers actually) and Grandma needed Mom and her siblings to work in the family diner. Mom cried when she was told she could no longer go to school. She loved learning.

My mother was ecstatic that not only would I graduate from high school (the first ever in the extended families), but I had the ability to go to college! Immediately a vision and a purpose formed in my mother's mind. Her little girl was going to go to college, and she would do everything in her power to make it happen from that day forward.

Mom worked two and three jobs, whatever she could, to make ends meet. She would make whatever sacrifice was necessary to see me to this goal, but she also told me, "You have to get straight A's so you can get a scholarship, because I don't have any money to pay for college." Somehow my mom figured out that the only guaranteed road out of poverty was through education, and she was determined I would get there.

The school system wanted to skip me from second to fourth grade, although I was a small-for-my-age second grader. I had started first grade at the age of five; there was no pre-school, Head Start program, or kindergarten then. My mom didn't think it was a good idea to put a tiny seven-year-old into fourth grade, so she didn't allow it. I sailed through the rest of my school years, easily getting high grades. I was determined to get that scholarship ... for Mom.

I learned early on, however, that I did not ever want to get in trouble at school. One day in First grade, my mother told me to stay after school and walk home with my older sister, who was in third grade and had a later release time. I didn't know I was supposed to tell my teacher or anyone else about this. I just hung around the playground until my sister was ready to go. Another teacher saw me and told my teacher the next day. My teacher took me to the front of the classroom and bent me over her knee and spanked me in front of the whole class, which included some of my cousins.

I was embarrassed and humiliated and disgusted because I had not done anything wrong. When my mother heard, she was angry at the teacher not only for not believing me but for striking me without talking to her first. I swore to myself at the ripe old age of six, that I would never do anything in school to bring that type of humiliation and pain on myself again. I never ditched or cut classes for the next 12 years!

I went my merry way, excelling in school and enjoying the praise and adoration of parents and teachers for my successes. I was in spelling bees and math contests. I participated in Girls Athletic Association (GAA), and got straight A's and was in National Honor Society. I worked hard and received numerous awards and accolades. Yes, I did get that college scholarship to Arizona State University.

As I look back, I realize the tremendous sacrifices my mother made so that I could claw my way out of the poverty and never-ending work that had been her lot in life. When she worked in the school cafeteria, there were years when she would repair her white uniforms, re-sewing the splitting seams over and over again, wearing them until they were thread-bare. She did this so that I could have a new dress or gym clothes to participate in after school activities.

What I didn't see, however, was how much my sisters hated and resented me. I was my parents' pride and joy. My sisters felt that when I got something it meant there was less for them. I naively thought that we all had the same opportunities, and that they simply didn't want to do all the things I was doing. From what I saw my older sister didn't like school or want to participate in extra-curricular activities. She told me years later that she hated it when I got to ninth grade. She became "Paula's sister." My younger sister was 18 months younger than me but was in Special Education classes and could not have pursued my goals. My two younger sisters were seven and ten years younger. I'm not sure how much they understood Mom's vision for me; they just knew they weren't getting what they wanted.

I was also my Dad's pet. He was thrilled that he had a "smart" daughter. It made him feel good to brag about me. I also became the son he didn't have. I loved pushing the lawnmower, and I worked on the car with him. He taught me about carburetors, spark plugs, and oil changes. This didn't help my relationship with my sisters, but I went blithely on my way, doing my own thing, unaware that anything was wrong.

When I went to junior high, however, everything in my life changed.

Chapter 2

My World Expands

I was so excited to get to ride a bus to junior high school. It meant I was no longer a baby in elementary school. I was 11 years old and going to be a 7th grader! We called it Junior High. There would be multiple classes, many teachers and lots of extracurricular activities in which to participate. It was also the first time I would be exposed to kids who did not live in poverty.

The Air Force dependent children from Luke Air Force Base attended my Junior High and High School. They were like exotic beings to me. They had seen the world; they talked about places like Guam, Okinawa, England, Germany, Italy and Turkey. They wore pretty clothes and pretty shoes every day. They drank orange juice for breakfast every day. I somehow always equated this one fact – drinking orange juice – to being rich. For me, it was a pure luxury, something that I had never experienced as a normal part of life.

These kids were truly far from rich; I know that now. Once I joined the military and knew how the ranks were paid, I realized they were children of Staff and Technical Sergeants and were far from rich. They lived on base because it was free. To me, they lived like kings!

It began to dawn on me that my family's lifestyle was far from the "norm." My mother and father were practically illiterate. When dad did apply for "real" jobs, my mom would have to go with him to fill out the application paperwork. He would just sign it. He really wasn't qualified for anything except farm work and construction. He was so excited when he finally got a job operating a huge earthmover, instead of having to work as a manual laborer in the fields.

In junior high, I was doing well; keeping up my straight A average, but for some reason, I wasn't making friends with the kids from Luke. Finally, I walked up to one of the girls who seemed nicer than the rest, and asked, in my heavy country accent, "Why won't y'all play with me?" She replied softly, "Because you sound stupid." She didn't mean that my voice sounded stupid. "But I make good grades," I said. She pointed to her head. "But you _sound_ stupid." It took me a while to realize she meant that my accent made me sound unintelligent.

Realization washed over me. My country accent marked me as ignorant. They assumed every time I opened my mouth and this country twang came out that I was just plain stupid. From that moment I worked hard to get rid of my accent. I enunciated every word and listened carefully to how they talked. I wanted to be their friend. I wanted to hear their stories. I was starved for news about the big world out there. I also knew I couldn't achieve my mother's dream for me to succeed in college if people perceived me as stupid.

At home, I refused to work in the fields any more. "I'll do anything around the house—cook, clean—but I don't want to do that kind of work anymore," I told my parents. They agreed, mostly my mom, and I never worked the fields again.

I began to spend time in the homes of my friends who lived on the Air Force base. I observed how they talked, what they ate, and what they did in their spare time. I compared how they lived to how I lived and what I considered normal. It was amazing to me. They were members of the Base Youth Center where they socialized with each other, played games, and were on bowling teams. They were on youth bowling leagues and traveled to compete. It was such a bigger world. It was "assumed" they would go to college and become "professionals." They were not destined to be store clerks or cafeteria workers!

Junior High School opened my eyes to how my economic world compared to the rest of the world. For the first time, my mom's dream became my dream. When I went into high school, my mother was over the moon with excitement. Her vision was slowly becoming a reality. She lived her high school years vicariously through my high school years. If we needed anything she could provide, she would do it. She drove the pickup truck pulling our class float for the homecoming game, for example. She worked at the refreshment stand for our club fundraisers. When she was working at the school cafeteria, all my friends would go over and see her. Even though it wasn't "cool" to eat in the cafeteria, if she was cooking, we all ate there.

About the time I turned fourteen years old, it became clear to me that my father was an alcoholic. I also realized that my parents had a pretty rough marriage. When my dad came home drunk one night, I insisted on driving him to the hospital because I thought he was sick. He had taught me to drive out in the cotton fields when I was 12. My mother refused to drive him because she knew he was just drunk, not sick. I insisted on driving him and would have tried if she hadn't realized I was serious. She drove us all the hospital. They stitched him up because, according to him, he had fallen and hit his head. According to my mom she had hit him over the head with a pop bottle when he came home drunk. I can believe her, in retrospect. At the hospital, the doctor asked him to follow the light pen he was moving back and forth. My dad said, "I'll be happy to, doc, if we tell me where it is." The doctor looked at my mom and she knew my dad was faking it. I felt confused. I had been my dad's pet all my life and couldn't believe this was my hero. We took him home and he went to bed. Up to this point, my parents had been very good at hiding these problems from us girls.

Early one morning, after I'd had a late night at a school event, my mother woke me and ushered groggy me into the living room. "There's something I need to tell you. You're old enough now to know what's going on," she said, sitting on our worn sofa. I was sixteen. She proceeded to tell me that she had known for quite some time that Dad had been unfaithful to her, and he was an alcoholic. He was currently having an affair with a woman named Carrie, and Mom wanted him to leave.

But for my dad, his family was his possession. He knew he was a hick with a sixth-grade education, barely literate, and he was not going to give up anything that bolstered his sense of self-worth. He was the head of household and finally owned his own home for the first time, and that had huge meaning for his self-worth. It made him feel like "somebody." He said, "If you want to leave, you go right ahead, but I'm not leaving my house."

Once before, when she only had three kids, she had tried to leave him and move home with her mother. My grandmother refused to let her move in. She told Mom, "You made your bed; now you can sleep in it."

On the night she told me the truth about my Dad, my mother and I went out and found the bar where Dad and Carrie met. We confronted her. "You can have him! Please take him and get him out of our house and our lives," mom told her. Carrie didn't say anything. I think she was too stunned.

But Dad wouldn't do it. He insisted that Mom leave, thinking she wouldn't leave the home she'd worked so hard to get. We had finally moved out of migrant and the government housing projects when I was 13, and bought a little three bedroom cinderblock house. Our mortgage was just $72.00 a month; it's amazing looking back at how nervous we were each month wondering if we could make the mortgage payment.

Mom didn't hesitate. She loaded us all up and took us to Grandma's house and told her mother, "We're here and we're not leaving this time."

Several months later I confronted my father. He still considered me his pet and I thought he might listen to me. "You need to leave the house, Dad," I said. "We can't go anywhere. Your four children need the house (my older sister had left and gotten married at this point). Go live with your parents, please." I told him, "If you want to prove to Mom that you have changed your ways and still love her, do it from a distance. She will never take you back if you keep her out of her house." So he finally did move out of the house; in essence, I kicked my father out of his house.

Chapter 3

College Bound – Not so fast!

With Dad out of the house, Mom was happier than she had ever been. They didn't get a divorce at first because there was no money for a lawyer. I was happy too. We were still poor; we made use of everything we owned and rarely threw anything away. I was working at a five-and-dime store, helping Mom pay the bills, and taking care of my younger sisters.

I started working the day after I turned 16. I made $1.60 an hour, minimum wage in 1970. The water bill was $5.34 a month. Even though that doesn't seem like a lot of money, it was four hours of work on my part, and it was a great help to my Mom. Though the situation was tough on all of us, I learned the ability to adapt and overcome out of necessity.

We ate a lot of beans, potatoes, mac and cheese and onions during those years. The onions added flavor to the cheap, starchy meals we could afford. Thirty years later I learned that white onions are a tremendous help to the immune system. I was rarely sick growing up. I can only imagine that because of my mother's rigorous cleanliness standards and eating those onions, we stayed healthy.

At TG&Y, the five-and-dime where I worked, they sold fabric and I received a 20 percent employee discount. I would buy cloth and my mother and I would sew clothes for me and my younger sisters. I had learned to sew in Home Economics classes in junior high and high school. I taught my mom how to sew. It was the first time I owned clothes that had not been hand-me-downs from my older sister.

At first we had an ancient pedal-driven sewing machine from my grandmother. Eventually we were able to graduate and buy the least expensive Singer model available. Mom and I bonded over making those clothes. We were able to have new clothes.

Freshman year, I had issued a challenge to my mother. Since she hadn't graduated from high school, I said, "Mom, we are going to race to see who can finish high school first. You can get a GED and I'll get my high school diploma. The first one to finish wins, and the loser will have to buy the material and accessories to make the winner a complete outfit. Then we will make the clothes together!

When my senior year began, I reminded her of the bet. "Mom, you need to get started! It's my senior year and I'm close to finishing first!" She signed up for the GED classes offered at night at my high school, and she studied diligently.

About halfway through the year, I came home from some evening event to find her crying at the dining room table. Alarmed, I asked, "Mom! What's going on?" I hadn't seen her cry since the last time we couldn't afford shoes. She sniffed and turned anguished, reddened eyes toward me. "They ran out of money and cancelled the GED classes." I was astonished and so sad for her. She only had to finish the math class to be ready to take her GED test. I couldn't believe her dream to finish high school had nearly come true, only to evaporate because the public funding money had run out.

A moment later, a gleam came into her eye and she turned to me. "Paula, you could teach that class." I was barely seventeen years old. My mother's brother (my uncle) and some of my high school friends (a few years older than me) were in that class. They were now nineteen, had been juniors during my freshman year, but had not graduated. I gulped, "Wow, do you think they would let me?" Mom smiled, "It sure can't hurt to ask."

So I went to the principal and offered to teach the class. For free. Of course, he didn't turn me down! At age seventeen, I taught my mother, my uncle and my friends their GED math preparation class! By the way, I learned from this experience, "It can't hurt to ask!" A lesson I applied 30 years later in my life!

In March 1972, it was time for Mom to take the GED test. I was at work at TG&Y the day she took it. I was alone toward the back of the store stocking shelves in the toy department when she came around the corner, looking upset and forlorn. My throat tightened and my heart sank; I was crushed for her. I said gently, "Mom?"

Then she got the most beautiful smile I had ever seen on her work-worn face; she absolutely shone with pure joy. I had never seen her look so lovely as in that moment. I cried, "You passed!" She was so excited. "Yes, I did!" she practically yelled. It was the greatest bet I've ever lost in my life!

We hurried, laughing, to the fabric section in the front of the store. We chose her pattern, the fabric, accessories, ribbons, and buttons. I put it all on my employee account. I was so very proud of her and she was going to have a great outfit to show for it! We went home and immediately got started on her new pant suit.

When Mom got the GED certificate in the mail, you'd have thought she graduated with her PhD from Harvard. She was so incredibly proud of herself and that accomplishment. It was an enormously validating moment for her. She actually went on to attend Glendale Community College and had accumulated several college credits before her death in August 1973.

I was very lucky to have grown up with a plan to go to college. I had to work toward getting scholarships; but I was also involved in softball, cross-country track, and volleyball as part of the Girls Athletic Association (GAA) in my high school. I was also president of the Math Club and had been secretary of the junior class student council. I knew I could be successful in my life, in spite of growing up poor, because I had been validated. My intelligence had been validated; my capabilities had been validated. I used my school activities to experience and gain leadership skills.

So it seemed inevitable to me when I received an honor tuition scholarship to Arizona State University. I was going to use a combination of Pell grants, student loans, and probably a part-time job to pay for living expenses and books. My friend, Julie, and I were going to be roommates in a dorm at ASU. I graduated from high school in May of 1972 and the world was my oyster. I was excited, happy and proud. Mom was on cloud nine. We had done it! We had beat the odds and I was going to fulfill the vision dangled in front of me in the second grade.

Julie and I attended the freshman orientation at ASU and bought matching bedspreads for our dorm room. Then, about two weeks before it was time to check in, I began to get sick in the mornings. I suspected what was going on. My boyfriend and I had dated most of my senior year in high school. I graduated a virgin, but we figured, all our friends were doing it, so why not? After all, you can't get pregnant the first time you have sex, right? Well, I found out the truth of that old wives' tale.

I wasn't going to tell Mom; I knew it would shatter her. I thought I would go off to college and get at least a semester done and make plans from there. My mother would be devastated! I just didn't have the courage to tell her. Girls didn't go to college pregnant in those days.

But the real problem was that I was sick as a dog with morning sickness, and prior to that I never, ever got sick. Mom thought I was dying; it never even entered her mind that I might be pregnant. She insisted on taking me to the doctor, one we'd seen for many years. I urinated in a bottle and the nurse ran the tests. When she came back into the examination room, the nurse said, with no preamble at all and right in front of my mother, "Would you like the doctor to carry you throughout your pregnancy?"

I watched my mother age ten years right before my eyes. The nurse quickly realized this was unexpected information. She said, "I'll leave you two alone," and backed out of the room.

I could hardly meet my mother's eyes. "You know," she said softly, "I never would have expected this. Not from you." She shook her head and looked down at her hands in her lap. "You're too smart for this. Who was it?" I exclaimed, "Mom!" I had only been dating one guy for the last year, so I was shocked that she even asked. She said, "I suspected there was something going on, but I just didn't want to believe it."

All I could choke out was, "I'm sorry, Mom."

Before we left, the doctor and nurse, who were husband and wife, spoke to us. "Would you ever consider adoption?" the doctor asked. They had adopted their own children and knew other families who would love to have a child, but could not. "If you do want to consider adoption, let me know." But I could not even begin to think about giving my child away.

When we got home, my mother and I knelt and prayed, "What now, God?" We asked. We both realized that in 1973 there was no chance of me going to college pregnant. It just wasn't done. We called my sister Brenda in the state of Washington to tell her. She knew I had been sick and asked how I was feeling. "Well, I will feel a lot better in about nine months," I replied. "Oh, no," she gasped, then covered the mouthpiece. I could hear her muffled voice, talking to her husband. She got back on the phone. "Come to me," she said.

I called my friend, Julie, to tell her I would not be going to college. Instead, I went to live with my sister to have my baby. The plan was that after he or she was born, I would return to Arizona and figure out where to go from there. Abortion was not an option in those days. It was possible in California prior to Roe v. Wade. The mother of a friend, a nurse, didn't want me to give up my dreams. She begged me to let her go with me to California; she would make sure I was safe. But I just couldn't do it.

My sister had two little boys, ages two years and ten months old. One day the two-year-old, sitting in his high chair barely a foot away from me, kicked back so hard that the chair crashed to the floor before I could reach it. My nephew was hysterical, crying and screaming in pain. I too became hysterical. The incident replayed itself over and over in my mind; how could I take care of a new baby if I couldn't even stop a toddler from falling down? I felt so helpless and guilty that I had not prevented my nephew's pain. I was eight months pregnant at that point. The baby was very real and coming soon.

I also realized that I was 'poor white trash' in my own mind, unwed and pregnant, with nothing to offer a child. I was a stereotype. I would not have a college education. I would not have a job when I returned to Arizona. I had left a job making $1.60 an hour. How in the world was I going to take care of myself, let alone a baby? I had seen several of my friends and family members get pregnant out of wedlock and keep their babies, and it was not a happy picture.

I did not want to bring an innocent child into that desperate environment and life style. I didn't want to be poor white trash any more. My world had expanded and I had worked so hard to make sure my life would turn out so differently. I still felt sick with guilt every time I thought about sabotaging my mother's vision of a better life for me too. She had sacrificed so much for me for the previous decade. What a mess I had made of my dreams, just for sex. What an idiot. I called my mother and asked her to approach the doctor about adopting my baby.

By this point, my mother had a divorce lawyer. She had finally filed for divorce, and her lawyer offered to help with the adoption. He had a list of 15 families waiting for babies. We did what was known as a 'gray' adoption. A lawyer makes all the arrangements between the young woman offering the child for adoption and the family looking for a baby. The family pays all the medical expenses and attorney fees. I didn't 'sell' my baby. I received no money personally.

In March 1973 I gave birth to a baby girl. Three days later, the adoptive parents flew to Bremerton, Washington, to pick her up. I got to see her for those three days in the hospital. On the last morning, I kissed her on the nose and told her, "Be happy." I kept my sanity during those days and nights by repeatedly reminding myself how happy this husband and wife were going to be when they saw her and were able to take her home.

The couple had engaged a lawyer in Bremerton to handle my paperwork. When my sister and I went to his office on the way home from the hospital to sign the adoption papers, he kept looking back and forth between me and my sister. He finally said, "The adoptive mother was just here. She looks more like you than your real sister does." That actually gave me peace that the baby girl would physically blend into her new family. I left Bremerton three weeks later to return to Arizona.

No job; no plan; no dream.

Nothing.

Nothing but a vision.

Chapter 4

Sucker-Punched!

When I returned to Arizona I went back to work at TG&Y in Sun City. I had been a reliable employee, so they welcomed me back. I fell into my old life.

One summer day I was serving some customers at the cash register. An older woman spoke to me. "I've been watching you," she said. "How would you like to work with me at the Greyhound bus office?" It was across the parking lot from the store. She continued, "You are always so patient with the elderly people."

Once, as a young child, I had made fun of an elderly person, and my mom said quietly to me, "Please don't do that. I'm going to be an old lady someday." For that reason, I was always very patient and gentle with the retirees and elderly. We were in Sun City; there were a lot of older customers there.

I replied to her, "I'm sorry; but I'm leaving in six weeks to join the Air Force, but I do know someone you could hire." "Who's that," she asked. I smiled. "The person who taught me how to treat senior citizens. My mother."

The woman actually interviewed and hired my mother. So Mom became a Greyhound bus ticket agent. She was so proud and so excited. Finally, she wasn't just a store clerk or cafeteria worker. She would bring home her book with all the bus schedules and routes, (these were the days before computers) and we would role-play so she could learn her job. She would say to me, "Where do you want to go today, Paula?" I would pick out destinations like Chicago and Florida. She was so thrilled to have a job with advancement opportunities and maybe have a career of her own... thanks to her GED!

In April, when I returned from Washington, I had gone to an Air Force recruiter's office. Since my scholarship was given to someone else when I decided not to go to school the previous fall, I needed a new way to pay for college. I remembered hearing that the military would pay tuition on the G.I. Bill, so I went to the Recruiter and took the military entrance test, the Armed Services Vocational Aptitude Battery (ASVAB).

When I was in ninth grade, an Army female recruiter had passed me in the hallway on Career Day. We didn't speak, but I never forgot the image of how sharp she looked in her uniform. It was the first time I had seen an over-the-shoulder strap on a purse. I thought that was so cool. When I was struggling to find a new direction for my life that image came back to me. Since many of my friends had been Air Force dependents and I'd visited the Air Force base often for the previous ten years, the military seemed like a comfortable, safe place to go. They would pay for college, feed me, cloth me and train me.

When the recruiter had the results back from my ASVAB test, he called me back to his office. "You can be whatever you want to be. You're the only female who has passed the ASVAB tests to be eligible for a non-traditional role for women in nuclear weapons. How would you like to do that?" (Traditional jobs for women in the military at that time were limited to administration or nurses.) He had a quota to fill for women in non-traditional jobs, so he was thrilled when I came along. So I said, "Sure, why not?" I was mainly interested in getting the tuition money, and I didn't want to travel outside the country. I wanted to be near my mother to help with my sisters. All of the inter-continental nuclear bases were in the continental United States. I went home and said to Mom, "I joined the Air Force today."

She looked at me and said, "Can I come?" She wanted to join too. We immediately called the recruiter, but unfortunately, at 38-years-old, she was three years too old, beyond the age limit. We were both so disappointed. It would have been great for us to join the Air Force together and gone off to see the world. It would have made me feel a little less guilty about destroying both our dreams the previous year. "That's all right, Mom," I said. "When I get to my first permanent base, you can come, bring the girls, and be my dependents; and we will live happily ever after!"

Things were going so well. Mom had the new job with Greyhound, and in a few weeks I would be going to the Air Force. Her divorce was final, and she had actually finally accepted her first date in 22 years.

Since we worked at the same shopping center, Mom and I carpooled to work. She dropped me off at TG&Y on the morning of August 24th, and later, when she picked me up at the end of the day, she remarked, "Your dad has been calling me all day!"

Dad was supposed to have my younger sisters for the weekend so Mom had accepted the date for that evening. For some reason, he was pressuring her to trade cars, since, according to him, hers needed some work. Even though she kept telling him, "No," he kept pestering her about it. When we got home the phone was ringing. It was Dad again, and this time, Mom gave in. "Oh, screw it! If he wants the car, he can have it!"

That evening I had plans to go see my boyfriend, who lived across the street, play in a football game. His dad was driving his sister and me to the school, so we pulled out of the driveway just after my mother pulled out to swap cars with my dad.

As we followed her down the street, and she turned off the main road toward my grandmother's house, I had this horrible feeling I was never going to see my mother alive again. I spent the rest of the ride to the high school trying to figure out how I would take care of my three younger sisters, ages 17, 12 and 8. But then I shook it off, thinking I was being melodramatic and fanciful.

My boyfriend's sister, Cathy, and I climbed the bleachers to watch Chuck play. At about 8:30 p.m. he limped off the field, injured. He waved up at us, indicating he was all right, but he headed to the gym to be treated.

At 9:00 p.m., without any warning, I jumped up and cried, "Cathy, we have to leave." She frowned at me. "We can't leave, we have to wait for Chuck and for my parents to pick us up. Chuck is okay; he waved at us." I was adamant. "We have to leave right now!" We made our way down the bleachers and toward the parking lot. My heart was racing and I felt compelled to leave with all my being.

23

Cathy thought I lost my mind. We weren't even heading toward the gym where Chuck was. As far as she knew there was no car waiting for us; we would just have to cool our heels until her parents showed up when we could have been watching the rest of the game.

As we emerged at the bottom of the stairs and headed toward the parking lot, Cathy's father, Jerry, a man I'd known for five years and a Technical Sergeant in the Air Force, was walking toward us. His face was as white as a sheet.

As I approached him, I said, "It's my mom, isn't it? She's dead, isn't she?" He just looked at me, stunned. "Yes, she is."

It was a sucker punch straight to my gut. I nearly fell to my knees. Jerry held me and wouldn't let me fall. I wanted to scream at the top of my lungs. Everything inside of me boiled up and I began yelling, "No, no, no, no!"

The football team members came running off the field, thinking I was being attacked. I had to wave them off so they wouldn't jump Cathy's dad. "It's okay; it's okay," I gasped. To Cathy, I yelled, "Go get Chuck!"

Jerry said quietly, "You have to go home now. Your sisters need you." Brokenly, I replied, "I know."

To this day I don't know the identity of the woman who called my house and told my sister, "Your mother's dead," then hung up. (She's actually lucky I never found out. I would have torn her head off, literally.) The girls ran across the street to tell Jerry. He drove to the El Mirage police department to find out what was going on. El Mirage is a very small town of about 3,000 people. Everyone knows everyone. The police knew Jerry was a close family friend, so they admitted to him that, indeed, Mom was dead.

As Jerry was loading me into his car, I felt a crazy desire to run. I can only explain that I had the heebie-jeebies, and my gut feeling was to run just to get them out of me. "Please let me got and run a lap around the track," I begged Jerry before he started the car.

"No, Paula, I can't let you do that," he replied. I think he was afraid that I would go into some kind of hysterical fit and try to run away. I felt those heebie-jeebies for the next three years. I know it is because I was not allowed to run that night.

As Jerry and I approached the house in his car, my sisters came running out of the house, yelling, "Is it true? Is it true?" "Yes, it's true," I said. We all began to hug and cry out in the front of our house. Here I was just 18-years-old, with a seventeen-year-old special needs sister, a 12-year-old and an 8-year-old, whose father had just shot and killed their mother, and I was trying to comfort them. By this time family members were arriving at the house. They began to take us into the house. We just huddled and cried.

Carrie, my father's girlfriend, took Nina, the eight-year-old, home with her. My aunts took the other two sisters. I stayed with Cathy that night in her house across the street.

The hardest thing I had to do that night was to call my Mom's sister; they were best friends as well as sisters. When she answered the phone, I said, "Aunt Shelby, my mom's been shot." She replied, "How badly is she hurt?"

I wanted to yell at her, "What do you mean how badly is she hurt? She's dead!" At first it made no sense to me that she didn't know. I choked out, "She's dead, Aunt Shelby."

My aunt began to scream and yell, and her husband, Uncle Jesse, grabbed the phone, yelling, "Who is this?" I said, "It's me, Uncle Jesse, Paula. My mom is dead." He replied, "Oh, my God," and hung up.

In the middle of that first terrible night, I woke up at about two o'clock in the morning and just started to scream. When I had awakened in the dark, the horror of my Mom being dead washed over me. It was pitch black and I was disoriented and I just couldn't grasp the reality of it all. I couldn't hold it together any more. Cathy's family came running into the room; Jerry sent for a doctor and they gave me a sedative.

Exactly a week before her death, my mom and I had been sitting on her bed, talking as we often did. Referring to my father, she said, "You know this is not going to end well, right? One of us is going to die." We looked at each other. "I hope it's him" I said darkly. The horrible irony didn't hit me for months later.

The day after Mom died, we all reassembled at my house. My sisters were brought back and we all huddled together. Someone called my older sister, Brenda, who was in Washington still. I don't even remember how she was told and when she arrived. My Aunt Shelby and her husband were there to support us. Someone fed us. We began to make plans for the funeral and burial.

In the late afternoon on that first day, a police car arrived with my Dad in the car. He wanted to see us. He was not arrested. The police brought him because they knew my mother's family would try to kill him, literally.

I walked to the police car. Dad said, "I want to see my girls." I replied, "Not today, Dad. Not today. I just need you to leave." I knew we needed a few days of mourning before we had to face him. He agreed and the policeman drove away.

I learned much later that the story my Dad told the police was this: Mom brought the car to my grandparent's house, where he was living. She went into his bedroom and they began arguing over the car and who was supposed to have the kids for the weekend. Mom did not know if Dad found out about her date and was just trying to block it or if he had a date and did not want to pick up the kids. That is what she told me earlier that day.

Dad always kept a loaded Colt 45 pistol hanging on the bed headboard in an old-fashioned gun belt and holster. It made him feel like John Wayne in a Western movie, I think. Dad claimed that Mom said, "I've had enough of this!" and then she grabbed the gun and pointed it at him. She knew it would be loaded. He tried to wrestle it away from her, and it went off, killing her instantly, with a single shot going through her face between her nose and mouth.

My uncles, who were outside with Gramma and Grampa, heard the shot. My dad went running outside, yelling, "She's dead, she's dead. Oh my God, she's dead." I didn't learn this part of the story until 13 years after my Mom's death when I attended my father's funeral. My uncle, one of his brothers, told me the story. He had been there on that day.

My mom was just five feet tall; Dad was six feet. Since Dad was the only witness, I will never know what really happened. Do I believe my mother could have done that? Yes, I believe she could have been that frustrated after two decades of infidelity, drunkenness, pain, and suffering. It wouldn't even matter that they were finally divorced. He just wouldn't leave her alone to live her life.

One of the reasons she wanted to join the Air Force or at least join me at my new duty station was so she could finally get away from him.

Two days after Mom's death, my Air Force recruiter called me. He had read my mom's obituary and knew that Alene Gragg was my mother. I was scheduled to leave on September 29th for basic training. He offered me an immediate emergency discharge from my obligation. "Don't you dare!" I cried. "Get me out of here! Sooner if you can."

He gave me a new reporting date of September 11th. I used the next week to close up the house and put everything in storage. I returned the relatively new washer/dryer to Western Auto, since it was not fully paid off. I had so little time to do the final tasks to settle my mom's estate, what little there was of it.

She was only thirty-eight years old and she was gone.

One of the most shocking incidents for me during that few weeks of closing out her life was finding her personal calendar. She had appointments scheduled for the following weeks. She had plans that that would occur after her death. I don't know why that really bothered me. I couldn't seem to fathom why she would have life events planned after her death. Maybe that sounds weird. Of course she couldn't know when she would die, but it just seemed unbelievable that she would have written down appointments after August 24th. It was embedded into me on that day that you never know when life will end and life is truly short.

My father was never formally charged with my mother's murder. He went to jail every weekend for six months for illegal possession of a firearm. Dad married his girlfriend, Carrie, three days after Mom's death so that he could petition for custody of my sisters.

I was leaving for basic training so I couldn't fight him for them at that time. My Aunt Shelby did take my 12-year-old sister, Tammy, to live with her. She had a daughter the same age. Tammy stayed with them for the first year after Mom's death and then went back to my father and Carrie to be with her sisters.

On September 11, 1973, I got on an airplane to basic training with $20 in my pocket given to me by Jerry, my boyfriend's father. The best way to survive basic is to be numb. There was nothing they could throw at me that I could not handle. I just didn't care.

Chapter 5

The Common Denominator

I am embarrassed to admit that I have been married four times. I was married three times by the time I was 26 years old. It would be almost two decades before I would figure out why I kept getting married.

The first time I got divorced, I blamed all the problems on the other person. The second time, I figured the problems and fault was 50-50. But by the third divorce, I had to look in the mirror and admit I was the common denominator.

I'll have to go back to Basic Training following my Mom's death to really explain how three marriages happen in such a short time period.

When I headed to Lackland Air Force Base, Texas, for basic training we arrived at two in the morning, exhausted. At 4:30 a.m., these people dressed in funny Smokey the bear hats, came in yelling at us to get up and get ready for breakfast. We were yelled at and ordered around all day long during Basic. Frankly, it was rather nice to have someone telling me where to be, what to do, what to wear and when and what to eat. I didn't have to think, just do. I was still reeling from my mother's death, so I was actually grateful not to have time to think or feel the pain. For six weeks, I saluted smartly and did everything I was told to do.

I only had one altercation with another member of our flight because she refused to do her share of the chores. Whenever it was our turn to clean the latrine, she would lock herself in the toilet as if she had to poop. One day, she crossed her legs. I lost it. I started banging on the door and yelling, "No one crosses their legs when they go poop. Get out here and help us clean this bathroom!" She never tried that again. I think people were shocked at me because I had been so quiet before that.

I graduated Basic on my 19th birthday and left for my formal training base at Chanute Air Force Base in Illinois. It was my training school for nuclear missile maintenance. We went to school from six a.m. until noon. Then we had lunch and afternoon duties. After we were dismissed we would change our clothes and go to the Airman's Club to hang out. The guys would play touch football on the lawn out back. I would stand in the doorway with my soda, watching.

One of the Airmen, Tom, noticed my interest and waved to me to come out. He asked if I wanted to play. Sure, I did! I had been very athletic in high school and was eager for some exercise. I was able to play wide receiver and Tom was the quarterback. He never overtly hit on me; he was just very nice to me. We started dating and by December we were married, just six weeks after we met.

Despite all I'd been through, I was lonely and scared in Illinois. My mother's death had left me rudderless and wiped out my self-esteem. I had had such dreams of college and being a career woman, dressing in business suits and carrying a leather briefcase. That was all gone, and now I was in the Air Force in Illinois. Tom seemed to understand that I was alone and scared. I was tired of standing on my own two feet and carrying the weight of the world on my shoulders.

I think I believed if I was married, I would not ever be alone again, and he would be my partner at whatever bases we were sent. So Tom and I were transferred to our first duty station at Francis E. Warren Air Force Base, near Cheyenne, Wyoming.

I knew that my mother's vision for her girls included each of us getting at least our high school diplomas. So the minute I could, I went back to Arizona and stole my 17-year-old sister from my dad. I literally snuck into his house and took her away. She was willing to go to Wyoming with me by that time. Although she had minor mental disabilities, she had managed to get to her senior year of high school by attending Special Education classes. She graduated and even walked through the graduation ceremony in her cap and gown to receive her high school diploma. My mom would have been so pleased. She had always worried about what would happen to Sandy.

Sandy moved to Oklahoma after graduation and lived with my Dad's brother, our favorite uncle on Dad's side. She met her husband there. Tom, bless him, was wonderful to put up with this intrusion in our young marriage. He never fussed about her although she could sometimes be high maintenance.

Sandy was gone before I got pregnant with Chrystie, a year and a half after our marriage. I was working full time in the Air Force as a Missile Systems Analyst Technician and Tom was one of the maintenance technicians who repaired the equipment we would bring in from the missile sites. After six weeks of maternity leave, I found a wonderful lady who babysat children in her home, Debbie. She loved and cared for Chrystie as if she were her own child.

In addition to working full time, I enrolled in Laramie County Community College and began taking college courses. I never lost the dream of getting that college degree. I would get that degree if it killed me, just to honor Mom's memory and sacrifices. The Recruiter did not lie; the Air Force did pay for college classes. I began with basic classes, like English and Math. It felt good to make progress on my dream of a college education.

Tom and I were only married two and a half years, when I asked him for a divorce. He asked, "Who gets the TV?" I said, "You can have it." "Then you can have your divorce," he answered. The fact that he asked about the TV and not about custody of Chrystie solidified my decision that we were friends but did not have the same long-term goals.

Tom had held me many times while I cried my eyes out over my Mom. He always seemed to know when I just needed to cry. He never tried to solve my problems or dictate what I should do. I will always appreciate him for that.

I took Chrystie and moved into a small basement apartment in Cheyenne. I realized that I needed some help coping with Mom's death, my divorce and the enormous amount of anger I felt inside, so I went to the Mental Health clinic on base.

The counselor asked me, "Who are you angry at?" I answered, "My father." "Does he know that?" I had not spoken to my father since the day after my mother died. "Probably not, I shrugged. "He's oblivious. I doubt he knows that I hate his guts now."

The counselor leaned back in his chair. "So who are you hurting? If you're not hurting your dad, because he doesn't know you're angry, then who are you really hurting?" Wow. I realized that all the anger I was carrying around had been hurting my child, my spouse, my co-workers, and myself. That one little visit helped me let go of the anger. I didn't forgive my father, but I did stop carrying around all that pent up anger. I figured if I couldn't direct the anger at my father, I might as well let it go.

One day, about six months after my divorce, a co-worker and I were chatting in the hall at work. I said, "I'm going to ask out the next guy who walks by!" I was lonely. Bob walked by; and I actually asked him out. He accepted my invitation. I think he was startled, but he said yes.

We had been dating a few months when we had a really big fight. He stomped out of my apartment, and I didn't know if he was coming back or not. I started to feel very sorry for myself. I was already divorced by the age of 22 and I couldn't even sustain a boyfriend for a few months. My self-esteem hit rock bottom. I began to say to myself that I could never be loved and wasn't worthy of love. I started to feel like poor white trash again. I had been unwed and pregnant as a teen; I had given up a child for adoption; I was divorced and wasn't even close to a college degree. It all piled up in my head, and I began to think of just ending it all. Suicide.

I had previously dropped a large piece of furniture on my foot and had a bottle of codeine pills. I had only taken one of the pills. I started thinking about just taking all those pills and ending it. I called Debbie and asked her if she could babysit Chrystie overnight if I brought her over right then. It was about 6:30 p.m. at that time. Of course she agreed.

I packed a little overnight bag for my 15-month-old daughter and took her to the babysitter, fully expecting to be dead that night. I dropped her off and did not give off any clues to Debbie that it would be for more than just that night. She had babysat for me before when I wanted to spend the night with Bob.

After driving back home, I went to the medicine cabinet and consumed all the pills in the bottle. I laid down on the bed and just let my mind go blank. After several hours, I began to feel very woozy. I realized the pills were starting to work. I began to think about my baby girl, Chrystie, and realized, "Oh, shit, what have I done!"

I got up off the bed and drove myself to the Emergency Room at the Air Force Base. I walked into the ER, no one else was there; handed the guy at the front desk the pill bottle and asked, "What would happen if a person took 34 of these pills?" He looked at me and very quietly asked, "Would that person be your height and weight by any chance?" I nodded.

He said, "Oh shit! Come with me." He took me into an exam room and called the doctor. The doctor administered ipecac to force me to throw up the pills. The poor guy from the desk had to count all the pills to make sure they all came back up.

At about 11:00 p.m. I said I had to leave so I could get some sleep before I had to be at work the next morning. The doctor looked at me sadly and said, "Young lady, you're not going anywhere. You'll be staying with us for a few days."

I didn't understand at first, but he meant that I would be checked into the 'psych ward.' I spent three days there. My unit commander came to see me the next morning to ensure I was all right. I was mainly embarrassed. He told me not to worry about anything and just get well.

I had three days of counseling and the doctor finally declared my suicide attempt to be a 'melodramatic gesture' to get Bob's attention. He released me to go back to work on the morning of the fourth day.

No one would tell Bob where I was or what was going on with me. He became worried. When I returned to work, he came to see me at my desk. I think he realized how much he cared about me then. Bob and I made up and began to date again.

Soon after that I got military orders directing me to transfer to Omaha, Nebraska. My old nemesis, low self-esteem, reared its ugly head again. I didn't want to go alone. I was afraid, and I was a single mom of a 15-month-old. Bob couldn't be transferred with me unless we were actually married. I have to admit, he was not keen on getting married. I think one of our commanders actually talked to him about it and convinced him to marry me. We were married in October, 1976, and moved to Offutt Air Force Base, in Omaha, Nebraska.

In retrospect, it was very wrong of me to insist on marriage and to drag Bob to Nebraska. I should have listened to him and should have accepted that he didn't want to get married. My first clue that we were not going to make it was that first Christmas. He chose to go visit his buddies in Wyoming instead of spending Christmas with me and Chrystie in Omaha.

I found out after we got married that he used illegal substances, but he kept that fact from me for the six months we were dating. We lived in two different homes in Wyoming. He would come over to pick me up for our dates and drop me off again at my place by 9 p.m. I thought he was such a gentleman with old-fashioned values. The truth was that he would drop me off and then go out to party with his buddies. Once we lived together in Omaha, he was very open about the substances and kept them in our house. This made me a nervous wreck. We were both on active duty and if he had been busted, I would have been guilty by association. I couldn't concentrate at work; I started making mistakes. After eight months, I issued an ultimatum, me or the drugs. He chose the drugs.

Chrystie and I moved into a two-bedroom apartment near the base. I went back to Arizona and stole my next younger sister, Tammy, and brought her to live with me. I wanted her to finish high school. She was having serious problems with her step-mother being abusive to her. I filed for legal guardianship of her and won. My dad did not protest at all.

She went to school and would babysit Chrystie when I started working a second job to make ends meet. I lasted six months working two jobs before I was too exhausted to keep it up. I was a cocktail waitress and began to drop drinks on customers because I was so tired. I quit before I could be fired.

Tammy lived with me for two years, then graduated from high school and married a military man. She traveled the world with him, went on to get some college credits, pursued her own career and settled down in Florida.

At the same point I was having marital problems with Bob, and I was also having trouble at work. I let my emotional distress spill over to my job. My boss, a Major, finally had had enough of my disruptive presence and "fired" me. He transferred me to another building as a desk clerk. He wrote a very negative performance evaluation on me and it went into my permanent record.

It was a horrible time in my life, but I did not consider suicide again. By this time, I was responsible for my sister and my baby girl. I could never make that choice again; I dug deep inside for the strength to stay alive to feed my girls and provide a home for them. They became my reason for living.

Third Marriage ... and divorce

I am either an eternal optimist or a flipping idiot! Who in the world would want to get married AGAIN after two divorces? When I am being flippant, I tell people my first two marriages were short-term leases, and I didn't renew their options. That statement is followed with I have really only been married two times, the third and fourth marriages.

Merritt "Beau" Francies came into my life when I was 'fired' the first time and moved to another building on Offutt Air Force Base. It is a military tradition to assign a sponsor to all incoming new people to help them get settled into the base and their new organization. My boss assumed that 'Merritt' was a girl's name so I was assigned to be his sponsor. When 'Merritt' reported for duty, however, he was NOT a girl. Since I was the first person anyone met in the organization, sitting at the front desk, the new recruit reported to my desk. When I glanced at his nametag, Francies, I burst out laughing. He was not amused. My boss decided I could still be his sponsor, so I showed him around the base and got him checked into his lodging quarters. He told me he preferred to be called 'Beau.' I would like to say, "and the rest is history" but it didn't really work out that way.

I was still married to Bob when I met Beau. They actually became friends and hung out together. After Bob and I split up, I moved into an apartment with my sister and daughter. After my sister got married, I invited a roommate to move in with me. At this time I also began a part-time job to help support my daughter and myself. My roommate offered to babysit. There wasn't a lot of time for dating.

Beau and I did manage to go out for a while, then broke up. I began to date a gentleman who was stationed at another base. He actually asked me to marry him so that we could be assigned to the same base. Beau found out about the marriage proposal and on New Year's Eve, 1978, said to me, "Don't marry him, marry me." I said, "Yes."

We planned to wait until the following Christmas to get married. Beau wanted a large, lavish wedding. He wanted to do it right. I was happy to wait and experience a real wedding for the first time. Six weeks later I found out I was pregnant. I have to be the most fertile person on the planet! I actually had an appointment for an abortion, but just couldn't do it! I told Beau, "I can't do this! Even if you no longer want me, I am keeping the baby." We eloped to Las Vegas on March 7, 1979. Alex was born in October.

I think Beau never forgave me for cheating him out of the big family wedding. We had issues right from the beginning of the marriage. He even suspected that maybe the baby was not his. For the first nine months of Alex's life, Beau kept him at arm's length. At 10-months-old, Alex's hair began to curl just like Beau's. That's when Beau finally claimed him as his own. I resented Beau for not believing me that Alex was his son, and built up a wall around my own heart.

We stumbled through our marriage, trying to figure out how to do it right this time. I had been accepted to the ROTC program at the University of Nebraska at Omaha, at the same time Beau was accepted to cross-train and become an Air Traffic Controller, a long-time goal of his. We were both about to achieve our dreams. Then I found out I was pregnant with Cynthia, our second child. Once I was medically disqualified from ROTC, the Air Force decided it was time for me to be transferred ... to Ramstein, Germany! Beau was away at technical training in Mississippi, and I was going to have to go to Germany with three children, alone. I elected to leave the Air Force and stay home.

During our marriage, I continued to attend college part-time one or two nights a week. I was determined to get my Bachelor's degree. I owed it to my Mom. Beau was assigned to Williams Air Force Base, Arizona. I transferred my credits to ASU and finished my final courses between 1981 and 1983. Finally, in May, 1983, ten years after Mom's death, I graduated with my Bachelor of Science, in Communication, from Arizona State University. That night I took a dozen red roses to my Mom's grave, and said, "This one was for you, Mom."

I was fired from my job at the Phoenix Air National Guard base six weeks before my graduation. I had tried to get my chain of command to understand that my supervisor was derelict in his duties. Now, anyone with any sense would know that going over your boss's head and complaining about him all the way up to a 2-star general, is not a very smart thing. It didn't take long for my boss to realize what was going on. I was also on a one year probation period for the job and was only at month 10. The boss really didn't need any particular justification to fire me since I was on probation. So he did. I went home and got drunk. That firing did push me into my Master's program at ASU. I needed the money to help support my children, and the GI Bill paid a living expense as well as tuition and books. In addition, ASU gave me a Graduate Teaching Assistant's job to teach two classes, which in essence set me on the trail to become an adult educator.

Over the next five years, things were bumpy in the marriage. For me, I was moving into academia and the professional work world. Beau was happy to be a high school graduate, with his boat and motorcycle for amusement. Our vision for the future did not match. I was determined to build enough credentials that I would never be poor again. I was also determined to create a lifestyle that ensured my children would go to college and be members of the middle class, and never know poverty.

In 1988, Beau was being transferred to California. I didn't go. At one point, Beau and I went to the pastor of our church and asked to be referred to a marriage counselor. Dr. Earle was perfect, because he was not only a certified family counselor, he was an ordained minister. Beau asked the counselor if I could just be given a pill and be cured. He refused to go back. I went twice a week for 18 months.

The Serenity Prayer

God grant me the serenity to accept the things I cannot change;

Courage to change the things I can;

and the wisdom to know the difference.

One day at a time!

Chapter 6

Sucker punched ... again!

For eighteen months, Dr. Earle, my counselor, and I worked hard on my emotional baggage. I was now a three-time loser in my mind. I had given up a child for adoption. I had been fired. Although I was an A-student at college, I could not seem to get my life together. We used the Twelve-Step program for Adult Children of Alcoholics as the core of my treatment. I had a lot of issues to process.

Before I began my mental-health program, and before Beau and I split up, I was teaching as a Faculty Associate at Arizona State University-West in Glendale. As I drove to work one day in 1987, I heard a voice telling me, "If you don't make peace with your dad, he'll die and you'll regret it for the rest of your life." We had not spoken since Mom died, thirteen years earlier. It sounded as clear as speaking to a normal person, but there was no one else in the car.

When I got to school, I found a pay phone and called my grandmother. I had no idea where my father was living. She burst into tears when I explained why I'd called. "He's been waiting for this phone call for thirteen years!" I told her to have Dad call me when he returned from Oklahoma, where he was visiting my uncle.

Dad called me promptly when he returned home. He lived just two miles from where I had been teaching for years. We met at a little pizza place near campus.

He brought his third wife with him, and he showed me a brand-new baby diaper, obviously never used, snow-white and with its original folds. "This was your baby diaper. I've kept it all these years," he said. Pity surged through my heart for this broken, alcoholic man. He expected me to believe the story of the diaper; it was incredibly sad. The leftover feelings of anger, disgust, and disdain evaporated. All that was left was pity.

I gave him a picture of my family, and invited him to come to Mesa and meet his three grandchildren. He said he would like to do that. He never came. We never spoke again.

Six months after that meeting, I got a call from my cousin. My father had been killed in a car accident. He was at fault. His blood alcohol level was three times the legal limit.

As I signed out of work the day of the memorial service, wearing a black dress, a co-worker laughingly asked me if I were going to a funeral. I answered, "Actually I am. My father's." She turned pale as a ghost. We realized at the same moment that I had told her about the voice six months earlier. I yelped, "I did tell somebody! I did tell somebody!"

At the service, I chatted with my aunts and uncles about my dad. One of my uncles said, "If somebody could have helped him, it would have been you. You were the only one he ever paid attention to. He talked about you all the time. He kept track of your career through other people in the family. He was so proud of you."

Dad had so longed to be somebody. Another uncle said, "I don't know when your dad began to believe his own tall tales." They were tales of working undercover for the FBI, being an undercover police officer—had he expected other people to believe them too? He had big dreams, but no skills to implement those dreams.

Apparently, I inherited my ability to dream, and dream big, from my father, and the perseverance to make my dreams come true from my mother.

Back when my mother died, I considered myself an orphan. I really lost my father then, too; there was no thought in my mind of reaching out to him and healing that relationship until I was essentially commanded by that voice. Thankfully, I heeded the voice, or I would have had even more unfinished business to process once I began therapy a couple of years later.

Dr. Earle and I identified three areas that were the foundation of my problems:

1. I kept getting married and getting involved in relationships because I needed external validation to feel good about myself.

2. I was trying to replace my mother, trying to regain the sense of family and security I once had.

3. I was angry with my mother for leaving me. Though this made no sense at all intellectually, because I knew Mom's death was not her fault, the anger was still there. To a hurting child, it doesn't matter why a parent is gone; it just hurts. The child is angry with the parent for leaving.

My self-esteem, which I had in spades before my mother died, was non-existent at this point. Beau had said to me, "For someone so smart, you are so stupid." That quote summarized my life at that point. I was beaten down, and I did stupid things.

For example, I was fired two-and-one-half times. How was I fired half a time? I realized it was coming and I quit before I could be fired! I was self-sabotaging my career, my family, and my marriages. I had already attempted suicide, in essence abandoning Chrystie. I had lost my job on active duty and at the Air National Guard base in Phoenix. I had been counseled about my performance at my civilian job, so I quit first; and I was a three-time loser on the marriage mart.

Dr. Earle started my counseling by having me write the words, "I am whole and complete all by myself," five times a day for months and months. I had to turn in this homework twice a week until I began to believe it. I learned through that experience that 'God don't make no junk.'

The good doctor also helped me process through the anger at my mom, and he had me write a letter to my dad, even though he was dead by this time, pouring out all my feelings about our relationship.

42

Beau had transferred to Beale AFB in California by this time. Because he was single, he was back in a dorm, sharing a room with an Airman. "I can't do this," he told me over the phone. "I've lost my identity as a head of household. I've lost my family; I've lost my children. If I get custody of Alex and Cynthia at least I can live in base housing and have a home again. At least you would have Chrystie."

I discussed the situation with Dr. Earle. I still had a lot of work to do on myself. Beau was a great father. He was the cook, the homebody, and the decorator of the home. I truly believed he would take good care of the kids, then eight and nine years old. It would help him get back his identity and his self-respect. I would see them several times a year, and they would stay with me every summer.

After a lot of prayer, anguish, and tears, while locked in my bedroom closet so the kids could not hear, Beau and I agreed to have the kids live with him. We met at Disneyland and I handed off my two children. I cried all the way back to Arizona. I would learn many years later the devastation that choice had on my two youngest children.

I "graduated" from Dr. Earle's program on March 21, 1990.

Two days after my "graduation" from my work with Dr. Earle, David Penson came back into my life. We had met six years earlier when I worked at the Air National Guard. Two days earlier, he had heard my voice on a radio commercial for the City of Tempe Community Services department. I was working in public relations at the time. He heard, "This is Paula Francies for the City of Tempe...You too can sign up for tennis leagues..." Dave looked me up in the phone book, where I was listed as "P.F. Francies." He figured that indicated I was single, so he called me on a Friday evening. We met that Sunday and have been together ever since. I call him my graduation present!

Professionally, I was doing fine, but I missed serving my country. The Air Force had saved my life. It gave me purpose, it gave me an education—the things my mom wanted for me. I had taken a five-year break from the military. When Operation Desert Shield began to gear up in the summer of 1990, I called the recruiter. I could get back in, but I had to start at the beginning and take the ASVAB again.

I joined the Air Force Reserve at Luke AFB. I could not go back to the Air National Guard because my significant other, Dave, was the Chief of Staff at my old unit and would have been in my chain of command. I was excited to be back in uniform! I was able to go from Staff Sergeant to Senior Master Sergeant in six years because I had finally figured out how to be a good employee, a good worker, and not to be shy about using my intellect and letting it show.

My relationship with Dave was going well, my kids were thriving, and life was finally on an even keel. Then in November, 1992, I was offered a job on Coronado Island, California. It was an offer I could not refuse. I would get to teach the senior leaders of the Navy and Marine Corps in one of the most beautiful places in the United States.

Dave, of course, needed to stay in Arizona at his job, so we kept up our relationship long-distance. He even agreed that Chrystie could live with him to finish her senior year of high school. The drive was not too bad; six hours each way, so every few weeks I would come home to Arizona.

Late one night, I was returning from Arizona to California when I had a terrible car accident. The car in front of me had no lights on, and I rear-ended it dead on without slowing down. The driver, a single woman aged 30, was not wearing her seat belt. She was thrown through the windshield and died immediately. My neck snapped with a torn ligament. My life was saved by my seatbelt.

When my car stopped spinning, I sat perfectly still in my car with my hands resting on my thighs. I was afraid to try to move. What if I could not move? Finally, I began to wiggle my fingers. Then slowly moved other pieces of my body. Eventually, I eased myself out of the car. I looked around and could see nothing in the pitch dark. I was literally in the middle of nowhere. I finally noticed the other car about 50 yards away. There was no movement inside or out of the car. I was terrified to look inside. I slowly crumpled to my knees. My neck was on fire. I did not know what to do.

After some time a face came even with my own. The paramedics had arrived. I learned later that they had been returning from a hospital run and noticed the shattered glass on the freeway. They drove backwards on the freeway until they saw our cars in the median. One paramedic went to the other car; one came to where I was kneeling.

"Are you hurt," he asked. I replied, "My neck." He told me to stay still, went to get the gurney and then prepared me for transport to the hospital in El Centro, California. The accident occurred at about 9:00 p.m. After I was examined and x-rayed, I began to ask about the other driver. The nurse just said, "Let's worry about you first, okay." I let it go. I had not been drinking at all, and apparently, it was obvious to the hospital staff that I had not been drinking because they did not take blood. One doctor said, "Well, you can thank your seat belt for your life," as he noticed the seatbelt rash on my neck.

Finally, when I asked at 1:00 a.m. what was happening with the driver of the other car, they admitted that she had died instantly. I began to cry and asked if I could call my fiancé. Dave finally answered the phone, and I told him what had happened. He said he would drive to me.

While I was still lying on the hospital bed, a nurse asked me if I was a teacher on Coronado Island. I could not imagine how she knew that, but said, "Yes, I am." The hospital had notified the deputy commander of the El Centro Navy base because of the way I gave my birthdate: date, month, year. It is a military date. They then asked if I was military. I said, "Yes." The base deputy commander had attended one of the Navy classes I taught and recognized my name. He mobilized the base Chaplain to take care of me. When the hospital released me at 3:00 a.m. the Chaplain took me to a base lodging room. Dave picked me up there later that morning. After we went to get my belongings out of my damaged car, Dave drove me home to Arizona. I returned to work six weeks later after neck surgery.

I felt deep guilt for taking the life of another human being. Someone was dead and there was no one else to blame except me. My car hit hers from behind. I thought, "My God, how can I ever atone for this?" The police report stated that I should be charged with involuntary manslaughter. I would have to do jail time. At the time, I was paying child support for Cynthia and Alex; Beau relied on that money. How was I going to help take care of my children if I was in prison? What would happen afterward? Would I ever work again? Would I lose my military career?

I wanted to curl up into the fetal position and wait for someone to tell me what to do, but I needed to do something to figure out how to take care of my children. I had nothing to lose to ask a few questions of several government agencies.

Since I was a certified teacher at the Community Colleges of Arizona, I approached the Department of Education. "If I go to jail, may I teach classes inside the prison to the inmates so they can get college credit? Could you send the salary to my children?"

The answer was, "Yes, as long as the Department of Corrections says it is okay." When I called the Department of Corrections, they also agreed; it would be beneficial to have a certified teacher available to teach classes inside the jail.

Then I called the Major who knew about personnel policies and procedures at the Air Force Reserves. "If I go to jail, can I come back?" I asked. He said, "I've never been asked that question before." He did some checking with the headquarters policy office, and the answer came back, that yes, I could return to my old job, as long as my conviction had nothing to do with my job specialty. For example, you could not be convicted of finance fraud and work in the Wing Finance office.

I was relieved to have everything in place to take care of my children, and was now ready to serve jail time. I spent September 1994 to January 1995 waiting for someone to decide my fate. On the morning of January 7, I got a call from my attorney.

"Paula, are you sitting down?" *Here it comes,* I thought. *I am going to jail.*

"The family of the victim has decided not to press charges." "What does that mean?" I asked, uncertainly. He calmly replied, "The police aren't going to either. The charges have been dropped." "What are you saying," I asked. He replied, "It means it's over, Paula. It's over."

I politely said thank you for the call, hung up the phone, put my head down on my desk, and sobbed like a baby. I repeated, "Thank you, Jesus. Thank you, Jesus" over and over. I could only guess that because I had let go and said, "Lord, thy will be done," and was willing to go to jail to face the consequences of my actions that God decided that I didn't need to go to jail. I wanted to scream out, "I'm not going to jail! I'm not going to jail!" It was such an amazing relief. But don't ever forget, what goes around comes around.

C³VS

Circumstances -> Choices -> Consequences -> Victory -> Success

*For all of us will endure the <u>circumstances</u> presented to us in life. We have free will to make <u>choices</u> in response to those circumstances.
We reap the <u>consequences</u> of those choices (both positive and negative).*

**If we have chosen well,
we will nurture resilience.
We will know <u>victory</u> and <u>success</u>.**

Chapter 7

Thy will be done, my ass!

A year later, in April 1996, Dave and I were married. In June, 1996, I found the daughter I had given up for adoption. I have one picture of my four children together. Life was finally sweet.

In October, 1996, Alex called me from California. He wanted me to come and watch him play in a football game for his seventeenth birthday. But apparently I had something important to do at work, so I said, "Son, I'll come later."

I never got to see him play in a football game. On October 9th, Alex was injured in a car accident. I got the call at 11:00 p.m. His back was broken in three places and his seat belt had severed his colon. Surgeons had to remove a foot of his colon.

Dave put me on the first plane the next morning, and I slept in Beau's spare room when I wasn't sleeping in Alex's hospital room. Alex was in the hospital for five days, and then was sent home to convalesce. He was in a plastic body cast so his vertebrae would heal.

I went to his school and got his books. I was a teacher by trade; I could certainly home school Alex for the next three months so he wouldn't be behind when he resumed school in January. I resigned from my job to take care of my son. He was in good spirits. Kids, coaches, and teachers came every day to the hospital and Beau's home to see him. He entertained them, not the other way around, as usual.

On October 23rd, Beau left for work, and I was cleaning the kitchen. I could hear Alex breathing very loudly, which was unusual, from his hospital bed in the living room. I stood in the doorway.

"Alex, stop that!" I said. I thought he was messing with me. "Shut up," he told me, and it was not a joke. I went back to cleaning the floor in the kitchen.

I never realized before how noisy normal breathing is. It is a part of everyday life and goes unnoticed. The only thing louder is the sound of no breathing at all.

Alex had stopped breathing. I raced into the living room, yelling, "Alex!" I grabbed the cordless phone and dialed 911. "Are you on base? Are you on Beale?" I screamed. "My son's not breathing! Are you on base?" "Yes, Ma'am, we're on base, what is the address?" the operator replied.

I yelled the address to the dispatcher, and slammed the phone onto the pillow next to Alex's head and began CPR. I kept yelling, "Where are they?" into the phone as I did the compressions I hoped would save my son's life. I didn't know that a blood clot had made its way into Alex's heart.

A Security Forces police officer arrived before the ambulance. "Do it; do it!" I yelled, meaning for him to take over the CPR; Alex wasn't responding and I was afraid I was not doing it right. I picked up the handset again, screeching, "Where are you? Where are you?" Then the ambulance arrived and the medics began to assess my son and start CPR. I went to stand at the end of the bed, massaging his feet and calves, praying, "Dear God, please, please, please…" I didn't even know what to pray for. I just kept praying, "please" over and over.

The EMTs tried to get me to leave the room, but I couldn't. I said, "If he's dead, I'm not leaving him. This is my last chance to be with him." Alex's dachshund, Willie, was under the bed, nipping at the medics' feet. I finally had to take him into the bedroom.

I had been trying to reach Beau, who was in the middle of a base exercise. 45 minutes went by, with the EMTs working on Alex. The medics announced that they were taking Alex to the hospital. I went outside to look for Beau, and he was running down the street. He couldn't get by all the emergency vehicles with his car.

I ran toward him. "He's dying," I screamed. "No!" Beau gasped. He ran into the house, took one look at his son, and came back outside. He could tell Alex was dead. We drove together to the

hospital. The medics had not said anything to us about Alex being dead, but they didn't put on their flashing lights or sirens. They knew Alex was gone.

Doctors met the ambulance, and they moved him into the emergency area behind a curtain. For a few minutes, nurses and doctors moved in and out of his curtained area. Then a doctor came to us and said, "He's gone." Beau and I moved behind the curtain. The plastic device that the medics had inserted into his mouth for CPR was still there. It looked grotesque, awkwardly holding his mouth open. Beau walked to the head of the bed and began to rub his forehead. He couldn't bring himself to touch him anywhere else or to look at his face. I leaned forward and kissed his cheek, saying softly, "Goodbye, son."

Out in the lobby again, Beau and I started making phone calls. Dave wasn't answering the home phone so I called my best friend, Jolene, and asked her to go to my house. The girls were at school, and I didn't want anyone to call Cynthia and tell her that her brother had died. Cynthia had moved in with me but knew all the same people that Alex knew back in California. Jolene intercepted the phone calls. I had trouble tracking down Dave; he didn't have a cell phone then. I asked Jolene to tell Dave, and to stay while Dave gave Chrystie and Cynthia the news. Jolene helped the girls pack for the trip to California.

Over the next few days, Beau's family members flew in to Sacramento. Dave made billeting arrangements for Beau's family, arranged vans for transportation, and organized food for 26 people for five days. Dave was the silent sentinel behind all of us, never bringing attention to himself, just doing what needed to be done. He allowed Beau and me to grieve and take care of arrangements for our son. Beau's father said to me on the last day, "He's a keeper."

Alex died on a Wednesday, and by Friday, the school had organized a memorial service. It was entirely prepared and run by the teenagers. I remember one teen reading a passage from the Bible, which said, "For I go to prepare a room for you in my Father's house." I had the thought that maybe God could get Alex to clean up his room. It was an irreverent thought during the service but made me smile as only Alex could do.

On Saturday, we had a service at the base chapel. We made 400 programs and we ran out. All the kids who had been on baseball, basketball, football, and soccer teams with Alex wore their jerseys. When they saw that it was standing room only, they got up and lined the sides and back of the chapel so others could sit down.

Alex had been a big man on this campus. At one point, when he'd been living with me and attending a large high school with thousands of students, he remarked, "Mom, I want to go back to California where I will be a big fish in a little pond, not a little fish in a big pond like I am here." So he went back to live with Beau.

I don't know how I got through those days. I spoke at the chapel service, describing how Alex would spend his first day in heaven. I imagined Alex waiting at the pearly gates for St. Peter. I imagined him leaning his tall, lanky, cocky self at the gates, asking, 'What's the holdup—let's get this show on the road!' He'd shoot some perfect hoops. He'd make miracle hail-Mary catches in the football end zone with all the pros who have gone before him. He'd knock perfect pitches out of the park. It would be a perfect teenage heaven.

Alex would saunter over to the steps where Jesus, God, and all the prophets were sitting, and make them all laugh with his Ace Ventura imitations. Finally, at the end of his first day in Heaven, he'd be pretty tired. 'Gentlemen, I'm going to be here for a long time,' he'd say, 'so I'm going to that room prepared for me in my Father's house.' Then, as he goes to his room, I remember thinking, 'Well, maybe God can get him to clean his room!'

Everyone in the church laughed. After they stopped, I said quietly, "That's what I was waiting for. Alex would want you to laugh! He would want you to enjoy life and achieve all your dreams.

51

Alex once told me that the thing he loved the most was making people laugh. So please, when you remember Alex, I hope you laugh."

Over 200 people, mostly teenagers, patiently waited in line to talk to me after that service. Every teacher he'd had from fourth to eleventh grade, every coach, and kids of every age, grade, ethnic group; tall, short; gay, straight--they all had Alex stories to share with me. Teachers told me they did not know whether to choke him or laugh with him when he acted like the class clown. Girls told me that Alex comforted them when they broke up with their boyfriends. One boy told me how Alex talked him out of quitting football camp— he ended up being a superstar on the team. There was not a mean or vindictive bone in his body. He had a pure heart. Alex had learned what he needed to learn, and God called him home.

Beau and I had to make arrangements at the funeral home to fly Alex's body back to Arizona for burial. I said to the director, "I'd like to fly Alex home on Sunday so we can bury him on Monday." He said, uncomfortably, "Planes don't fly on Sunday."

I thought he must be crazy. "I'm a traveling consultant. I travel practically every Sunday. Of course planes fly on Sunday." The man shifted in his seat. He looked down at his desk. "Not for freight."

I totally lost my mind! I jumped out of my chair and screamed, "My son is *freight?* My *son* is *freight?* Three days ago he was a living being and you've reduced him to FREIGHT?" I could not accept; I would not accept this final insult. That word was the ultimate injustice for all the pain and suffering I was going through. My beautiful, vibrant, adorable, lovable son had been reduced to a soulless piece of freight. I couldn't stand it. I couldn't endure one more minute in that office. I left Beau to finish the arrangements and went outside, where I cried out again and again, "My son is not freight!"

My son went home on Monday as freight, and we buried him on Tuesday, October 29, 1996. Eighty people from my military unit, along with friends and family came to help me bury my son. How do I know the exact number? A coworker came up to me and told me she had counted eighty people in attendance. She had noticed that it was the exact number on Alex's football jersey, draped over his casket, and thought I would like to know.

I have been a Christian since the age of four. I had believed Jesus loved me. When my mother died, I knew she was in a better place, and I was at peace with that. I was sorry for myself and my sisters and my aunts and uncles, but I was very happy for her. I had a wonderful image of her in Heaven that I carried in my mind to get me through the darkest days of missing her. I imagined her skipping through a field of grass and flowers without a worry in the world.

But when my son died, I was angry. I was livid! The only image of heaven I could see in my mind was huge roiling black clouds immersed with loud, crackling thunder and lightning. I yelled at God, "Thy will be done, my ass! How dare you! How *dare* you take my son? I've already had the 'significant emotional event!' My father shot and killed my mother; wasn't that enough? I've been fired three times and divorced three times! I killed another human being! Have I not suffered enough? Haven't I paid for my sins? Enough!" I cried out.

For the next two years, anytime I did bother to talk to God, I yelled and screamed at Him. For four months, I just wanted to die. I didn't want to kill myself, but I did want to just curl up and quietly die. I wondered, "Why bother? Nothing ever gets better. Life just gets worse and worse. No matter how good you are, no matter how good you've been, no matter how much you believe Jesus has forgiven you, He just keeps throwing crap at you." Nothing made sense. Why me, Lord! Why Alex! He didn't do anything! He didn't deserve to die! I didn't deserve to lose my son! Each day was a battle with myself and with God. I no longer had any hope. I only took two weeks off from work after the funeral. I had to go back because I was going crazy.

So I decided first, to ***get up.*** Get up, get out of bed, and drag myself to the bathroom. ***Suit up***, I told myself. Put on makeup. Get into clothes. Suit up and face the world. All I wanted to do was pull the covers over my head and scream out as loud as I could, "Go away cruel world!" Sometimes it took two hours to get to work when it should only take twenty minutes—because I would be crying so hard I'd have to pull the car over, dry my tears—because I still had to ***show up*** to life.

About four months after Alex's death, my daughters came to me. "Mom, we're still here," they said. "We still need you. We lost our brother too, but we're still here and we need the mom we had before—the optimist, the laughing lady, the hopeful and joyful Mom we've always had. We still need you." My daughters saved my life with these words, "We still need you."

Get up, suit up, and show up. I learned I had to do that every day for my husband, my daughters, and my co-workers. The alternative was to simply curl up and die.

When life throws you sucker punches, there's only one thing left to do!

Get up! Suit up! and Show up! each and every day to life!

The following is a letter I wrote to my son on what should have been his 35th birthday.

A letter to Alex

Dear Alex,

Today is 4 October 2014. You would have been 35 years old today. It shocks me when I realize it has been 18 years since your death, a year longer than you lived. It seems like yesterday. I still feel all the feelings I felt that day you died. Shock, denial, anger, depression. It took me two years to make peace with God over your death. I yelled at Him. Screamed at Him. Cried to Him. Denied Him. I just couldn't understand any kind of "God's plan" that could include your death.

You were so happy-go-lucky and just wanted to make people laugh. You didn't have a vindictive bone in your body. You were friends with everyone no matter their race, creed, color, religion, gender, age; it didn't matter to you. They all loved you.

You drove your teachers nuts being the class clown. They didn't know whether to love you or slap you. But they all acknowledged that you were special and pure in heart.

I wish we could have talked more. I remember vividly the few talks that we did have in those teenage years. I remember you were so hurt when your long-standing girlfriend broke up with you. I asked you, "Alex, did you do everything in your power to make her feel special?" You replied, "Yes, Mom, I think I did." "Then," I said, "This is not about you. It's about her." I remember asking you if there was anyone else you might have noticed in the past two years. You blushed when you admitted that you really liked her little sister, but she had been "out of bounds." [Call me crazy, but I thought it would be perfect justice if Alex dated his ex-girlfriend's little sister and lived happily ever after.]

Well, it wasn't very long after that conversation that you died. I don't know if you ever would have hooked up with the little sister, but I do know there were plenty of teenage girls who thought you were awesome and gorgeous. I remember the girls coming over to our house when you would spend summers with me in Arizona. One of them actually said to me while fanning her face, "Oh my God, he is so handsome; I want to faint." I just smiled and agreed. You never let your looks go to your head. I don't even know if you realized just how beautiful you were, inside and out.

You knew from a very young age that you wanted to be an NBA basketball player. You were growing like a weed and grew six inches the summer before your 12th birthday. I remember that summer before your 9th grade year of school. You would be going into high school that fall. You said very matter of factly to me, "Mom, I have a plan for my life."

I smiled and replied, "What's your plan, son?" You laid it out, without hesitation, step-by-step.

"In Freshman year, I have to concentrate on sports."

"Why is that?" I asked.

"I need the coaches to see me so that they will play me, Mom."

"In sophomore year I have to hit the books," he continued.

It made a Mother proud to hear that, but I did ask him why.

"Mom! He was shocked that I didn't already know.

"I can't just be a dumb jock. I have to get a college scholarship so I can go to college!"

He went on. "In junior year, I have to concentrate on sports again."

"Why is that?" I asked,

"Mom!" He said, very exasperated. "New coaches! The varsity coaches; they have to see me so they'll play me! That's also when the college scouts start coming to high schools."

"What do you do in senior year, then?" I asked.

"In senior year, I have to hit the books again. I know you can't afford to send me to college, so I have to get a scholarship."

He continued.

"In Freshman year of college, I have to concentrate on sports!"

I jumped in again, "I got this now; so the coaches will see you and play you."

He gave me a brilliant smile and said, "You got it!"

"In sophomore year of college, I have to hit the books again. Do you realize how few people actually make it into the NBA, Mom? I have to have a back-up!"

(Did I mention that you were only 12-years-old during this conversation?)

"In junior year ... ," he began.

"I know, I know," I interrupted. "You have to concentrate on sports so the coaches will see you and play you."

"No, Mom! I have to concentrate on sports because that's when the NBA scouts will be checking out the college kids."

I jumped in then, "And then in your senior year of college, you'll hit the books again, right?"

He looked at me very seriously and said quietly, "No, Mom. In my senior year I have to find a wife!"

I almost drove off the road! I had to fight really, really hard not to break into laughter, son.

"Why would you need a wife in your senior year of college, Alex?" I quietly asked.

"Mom. So many kids get into the NBA and they forget."

"What do they forget, son?" I quietly asked.

"They get into drugs, alcohol, and sex; and they forget. They forget that they're supposed to be a role model for kids like me."

At your funeral, Alex, hundreds of your friends waited patiently in line to tell me an "Alex story." They wanted to share with me how you affected their lives. The girls all told me how you were the go-to-guy to cry on a shoulder when one of their boyfriends would break up with them. You didn't take advantage of their vulnerability. You just listened, let them cry, and then made them laugh. They always knew they could count of you, and you never let them down.

The guys told me stories of how you kept them out of trouble or kept them on the team. One young man told me about the night you were all wandering around base housing at Beale Air Force Base. One of the guys wanted to get some spray paint and do graffiti on the empty houses. You simply said, "We don't need to be doing that. Let's go shoot some hoops." And they did. Another young man talked about wanting to quit the football team during summer football camp. He was laying on his bed thinking about quitting, and you just came over and started jumping on his bed around him, saying, "This is fun! Why would you not want to do this? This is fun!" The young man didn't quit and became a star player on the team.

The stories went on and on. I remember thinking, "Wow! What a cool guy my son was! I wish I'd known that Alex; the Alex that his friends got to see and know.

Well, Alex, maybe the truth is that you learned everything you were supposed to learn in this lifetime and you did it in just 17 years. I'm almost 60 and I don't think I have it nearly figured out like you did back then. There were over 400 people at your funeral, son. I know because we printed 400 programs and we ran out. Every teacher from 4th grade to 11th grade was there. All the members of all your sports teams, baseball, basketball, and football, wore their jerseys. When they realized there was standing room only, they all got up and lined the walls of the church to give everyone else a seat. I was so proud of those young men.

At one point during an especially emotional speech during the Memorial Service, something fell in the background making a loud pop that startled everyone. Your dad said aloud, "Alex!" and everyone laughed in agreement. We really did feel you were with us that day.

I remember praying that morning to say the right words when it came my turn to speak at your funeral. I remember being so angry and then realizing, it wasn't about me. It was about your friends, the teenagers. So I addressed my comments to them. I began by telling the audience that I would like to address my comments to the teenagers and that everyone else could listen if they wanted to.

I began to tell them how I imagined your first day in heaven. I could just see you leaning patiently on the edge of the pearly gates, being cool, knowing that someone would come to let you in. I said I could just imagine a gaggle of girl angels on the other side of the gates, whispering, "Alex is coming! Alex is coming!" ... and you were just being cool, nodding, and smiling that beautiful, amazing, impish grin.

I imagined that St Peter finally opened the gates wide and you strutted in, winking at all the girl angels as you headed past them on your way to the basketball court. As you passed you would have said, "Don't worry, ladies, I'll be here a long time!" Then you strutted over to the basketball court where all the great superstars of the past were there to greet you and bring you onto the court. You began to hit the sweetest three-pointers and never missed a layup.

After a short while, you said, "Thanks, fellas; I'll catch you later."

Then you headed over to the baseball field, and proceeded to hit the ball out of the park time and time again. After a while, you put the bat away and wandered over to the football field. There you proceeded to run a wide-right all the way down the field and catch the miracle catch on your fingertips. The crowd went wild. Finally, you waved goodbye and headed over to your Father's mansion where He had prepared a room for you.

You stopped at the front steps and proceeded to entertain all the saints, angels, and prophets. You had them roaring with laughter at your Jim Carrie, Ace Ventura, Pet Detective, imitations.

They were all clutching their sides in agony at your antics and you just smiled and bowed and said, "Gotta go now; not to worry, though, I'm gonna be here a long time."

I remember saying to the people in that church how I watched you in my imagination strut through the halls of the heavenly mansion on the way to your room. Then I remember thinking,

"Well, maybe God can get him to clean up his room."

At this point, everyone at your funeral burst out laughing, Alex. After they stopped I quietly said, "Ah, that's what I've been waiting for. Alex would want you to laugh. He would want you to get up, go on with your lives, and do great things. He would want you to dream big and do whatever your heart desired."

By the way, Alex, there were several adults in that line waiting to talk to me after the service. One father said to me, "I know you said you were talking to the teenagers, but it helped me too!"

We all went over to the bowling alley where the kids had put together a great party for you. There was good food and a big cake. People bowled and laughed, and it was beautiful and the perfect celebration of your life.

I miss you, son. There's so much you didn't get to do here on this earth, but there's so much you did while you were here. A friend of mine said to me a few months after your death, "You know, he was just on loan to you, right?" I realized, she was right. God loaned you to me and I know I didn't cherish you enough during the few short years I had you. So I ask your forgiveness for the time lost while I had you.

I try to forgive myself. God gave me such beautiful gifts when he gave me you and your sisters. I took you for granted and lost the chance to cherish you as you deserved.

I pray to see you soon. In the meantime, I cherish every day and try to make it mean something. I hope you're still having fun. I hope you're okay. How can you not be? Still, I would give a lot to have you here again for a while … just to love you a little better this time.

Please say hi to my Mom for me. I hope you've gotten to know her. She would have loved you so much! Chrystie and Cynthia are doing great! You would have been a wonderful uncle for their daughters. Their daughters, Sara and Trinity, are amazing! You would have had so much fun with them. Your dad is being a wonderful grandfather.

I love you, son! Wish you were here.

Love and hugs, Mom

****

How does a mom look back at that 12-year-old boy, who had the wisdom of a 35-year-old, and not want to just hug him and cry all over again? I was amazed. I had no idea he had such wisdom. I had no idea how much clarity he had about the world around him. Alex truly knew what he wanted and how he was going to get there. He knew what was important and he had a plan for his life.

By the way, Alex was working his plan when he died in his junior year. The results were what he wanted but not exactly how he planned it. He excelled in basketball, baseball, soccer, and football in his freshman year. He did concentrate on sports so much that he was placed on scholastic probation. He had no choice but to hit the books his sophomore year or he would not be allowed to play sports at all. At the beginning of his junior year, he was "BMOC!" Big Man on Campus! Everyone knew him at Wheatland High School. Everyone loved him.

He died two months later.

Chapter 8

I'm a Speck!

For the next few months, I got up, suited up, and showed up for work every day, and bit by bit, it did get easier. My husband arranged for us to go to England and Scotland a year after Alex died. My husband knew the first anniversary was going to be a bad day.

On the day that would have been Alex's eighteenth birthday, we were standing in Yorkminster Abbey. Archaeological digs had uncovered Roman ruins dating to 400 AD. There were markings on the walls underneath the abbey showing what structures were there in 400 AD, 600 AD, 800 AD, and when William the Conqueror won England in 1066. The abbey was built in the 1500s. I was awed by so much history. It was overwhelming to think that for over 2000 years, humans had inhabited this land.

Realization swept over me, and I turned to Dave, "I'm a speck! On the continuum of time in the universe, I'm a speck!" I am nothing. I can't make a difference. I'm insignificant. All these thoughts crowded my mind.

After our vacation, I went back to work, but I was depressed and discouraged. For so much of my life I had truly believed that, although I was just one person, I could make a difference, and I could change the world. But, really, I was just a speck.

I was right back where I was emotionally just after Alex's death. Again, I wondered, "Why bother?" Why not just quit work for good, sit on the couch at home, eat bonbons, wrestle the remote from my husband's clutched fist, and watch TV all day? Why bother working so hard and trying so hard, if I was just an insignificant speck?

For several months, I was devastated by this thought. But after a while, I began to think, what if George Washington had thought, "I'm just a speck; I can't make any difference, so I'll just stay over here in Mount Vernon." What if Abraham Lincoln had concluded, "I'm nothing but a speck," and had not bothered to hold the nation together through a terrible civil war? What if Martin Luther King had shrugged and said, "I'm just a speck; my dream and my courage aren't important to anyone else." What if Winston Churchill had not stood on England's shores, raised a clenched fist toward Germany, and vowed, "Not on my watch! Not on my watch! I don't think so! We will endure!"

So maybe most of us will not make "the" big difference in the world. I thought to myself, "I may not end up in the history books, but at least I can give it my best shot every day. I'm going to get up, suit up, and show up to life every day." After all, that's all we have: the choice to live our lives, to the best of our ability, every day.

Gradually it came to me that I needed to focus my life on serving others. I developed a personal daily prayer to help me stay focused:

"Dear Lord, help me to serve something greater than myself today; to serve the way You would have me serve this day. Lord, help me to teach everything I'm supposed to teach this day; and help me to inspire others to accomplish their full potential. Help me to learn what I'm supposed to learn, first about myself, next about the needs of others, and to learn about the subjects on which I'm supposed to be the subject matter expert. Help me to listen twice as much as I talk for I can't learn anything new if I am doing all the talking. Help me to love generously and uncondi-tionally, no matter race, creed, color, religion, gender, sexual orientation, age, height, weight, size or shape, or any other artificial demographic we insist on imposing upon each other; and most importantly, Lord, help me lead from wherever I sit."

For another year, I still struggled in my relationship with God. I was still mad at Him even while I was trying to serve Him and others. When Alex died, I felt as though huge weights were pressing on my back and my chest, squeezing my lungs constantly, like a cinderblock vise. I felt as though I could barely breathe for two years. As I read story after story about other parents losing children, I learned that I was not the only one who felt this way.

On the night of October 23, 1998, the two-year anniversary, I couldn't take it any more so I locked myself in my bedroom and went into my closet. I shut the door and sank to my knees. I began to pray.

"Lord, I can't live like this. I can't live angry all the time. I'm hurting everyone around me. You promised you would never give me more than I could handle. You promised you would never turn away from me. I know that it was I who turned away from you, not the other way around. I want to turn my life back to You. I am claiming your promises. Help me to work my way back, and please forgive me. I will never understand why you took my mother; I will never understand why you took my son. I will never understand, but I do accept that You have a plan. You see the bigger picture, and I cannot. I am putting my faith back in You, Lord. 'Thy will be done' has to have meaning for me again."

In that instant the cinderblock vise was gone. I took the first deep breath I had taken in two years. I could breathe again. I felt the burden of anger lifted, so I asked, "What would you have me do?" Over the years, the answer I have heard is simply this, "Tell your story. Wherever and whenever you get a chance, tell your story." I've often wondered if that's enough; is that all He would ask of me? Wouldn't he want me to start an orphanage or travel to under-developed countries? But no, the message has been consistent, just tell your story.

I will NEVER understand the deaths in my life history. I will NEVER understand God's will in those cases, but I definitely plan to ask lots of questions when I see Him!

I'm a speck!

On the continuum of time in the universe,

I'm just a speck!

But this is MY time! This is YOUR time!

WE own this time!

We own this!

If we abdicate our time,

then we deserve what we get!

Choose to make a difference!

From wherever you sit, you can:

Serve, Teach, Inspire, Listen,

Learn, Love, & Lead!

Chapter 9

Forgiveness

It has been almost impossible to forgive myself for the mistakes I have made.

When Beau wanted to sue the driver who caused Alex's accident and the hospital, I refused to have any part of it. "The driver of that car was a kid, and, more importantly, he was Alex's best friend," I pointed out. I knew what it was like to cause the death of another person, and I didn't want to make it any worse for that boy. I told Beau he could do whatever he wanted, but that I would have no part in any lawsuits.

I had no animosity toward anyone when Alex died. Well, except toward one person. Myself. Oh, and, maybe God. I had been the one to let Alex go live with Beau. I questioned myself, *"If only he'd been living with me, this would not have happened."* Well, of course that was not true, but I had to struggle through the feeling that I had been a bad parent, a lousy wife—definitely a lousy wife. I had three divorce decrees to prove it!

So, one day at a time—and I really learned the meaning of those words—one day at a time, I proceeded to put one foot in front of the other. I named and claimed again: "Get up, suit up, and show up every day to life." I realized that no matter how much I wanted to scream, "Go away, cruel world!" and curl up under the covers, I could not. I had to get up, suit up, and show up, because you cannot serve anyone from the fetal position.

I had also come to understand that every moment I gave in to the darkness and depression, every time I felt sorry for myself, and every time I yelled at God, the devil won. So I had to forgive myself for my past choices and not-so-stellar decisions. I made up my mind to say, "All right. So be it. Jesus does not base your future on your past mistakes—that is why He died for you. Thank God.

Did I still have my bad days? Of course. But I determined to do my best to keep the devil from winning any more. Does he win a few? Yes. Then I catch myself and turn back to God for strength, for hope, and for forgiveness. Acceptance and letting go of the past and former mistakes was easier the more I served others.

From October, 1998 to February 2001, things were going great. We were living in Texas and I was working hard in my civilian and military jobs, and enjoying my family. Chrystie and Cynthia came to live with us and go to school nearby. Cynthia was studying vocal performance at the University of North Texas, and Chrystie was working on her public relations degree at the University of Texas at Arlington.

On February 19, 2001, however, I got the kind of news everyone dreads. "I think you have adenoid cystic carcinoma," the doctor said. I replied, "I don't know what adenoid means. I think cystic means cyst-like. But I sure as hell know what carcinoma means. You're telling me I have cancer!"

Of course, it was a three-day weekend and I couldn't get to my primary doctor until the following Tuesday. The doctor asked me if I could drive home. "Sure, sure," I answered. "I am just going to stay in denial until I get home."

I stumbled out of the building and got into my car. I called Dave to tell him, "The doctor thinks I have cancer, but don't tell the girls yet. Let me get home and get my story straight, then we can figure out how to tell them." But when I got home, both girls' cars were in the driveway. *Gee, thanks, Dave,* I thought.

I went in the door and sat down in the easy chair in the living room. Cynthia sat down at my feet. Looking up at me, she asked, "Should I be worried?" I thought for a minute. "Let's not," I decided. "Let's choose not to be worried." She said, "Okay!" and bounced up and headed back to school. Now, that's faith!

I 'chose' to exercise absolute faith. *Let's choose not to worry.* We can worship or we can worry; we can have faith or we can have fear. Those two options are diametrically opposed. You cannot do both at the same time.

But the next time I was alone, I looked up to the sky toward God and burst out laughing. "Really? Really, God?" I thought He had already gotten my attention! But I guess I was still trying to assume I was in charge of my life. He literally slapped me in the face (the location of my cancer); and this time He had my entire attention.

The cancer specialist gave it to me straight. "This cancer is slow-growing, high grade, and it has no known cause and no known cure. We can treat you with surgery and radiation now, but it will come back in two to twenty years. When it comes back, it will be in your brain, spine, or lungs."

It was a defining moment. I had a two-to-twenty-year life sentence. What was I going to do? Well, if I only had two years, I'd stop working and start on my bucket list. Trouble was, I did not really have a bucket list. I just wanted to work. I wanted to serve. I wanted to have an impact, be it big or small. So I turned it over to God. "All right, Lord, I can't control this. I can't do anything about it. So, show me what you got."

Initially, the doctor told me my face would look like I had a stroke for about eight months. My daughters and I had professional photographs done the day before my surgery. When I came out of surgery, I asked my husband, "How's my face." He took his time and carefully searched both sides of my face. He replied, "I can't see any difference." I asked for a mirror. Miraculously, the surgery left no ill effects from having my nerves severed. Following the surgery, I had 40 radiation treatments, once a day, Monday through Friday. I also went once a month to the doctor for checkups for a year, then once a quarter, then twice a year, and for many years now, I have gone once a year. I am 15 years cancer-free. On my initial 2-to-20 year life sentence, I still have five years to go. Every day is a gift.

Chapter 10

Military Career Notes

Some people are able to bounce back after life has thrown them some major curve balls, and other people simply give up, lie down on the couch, and wait to die.

My mother's vision—and it was nothing but a vision—of my life being more productive, easier, more comfortable, and happier than her own, was the beginning. She instilled in me the desire to strive for something more, and the work ethic to make it come true. I learned to look for the gifts inside each hard lesson I suffered.

It's not that I never failed. For example, I was a Staff Sergeant (SSgt) for fourteen years. How could something like that happen to a smart, hard-working woman like me? Easily ... through self-sabotage.

At first, I was doing phenomenally well in my career. I was the youngest person ever to go to Non-Commissioned Officer Leadership School at age 21. I graduated second in my class of 108. I cruised along triumphantly, within three years being promoted "below the zone" (i.e. ahead of my peers) to E-5 (Staff Sergeant). Then I stalled and remained an E-5 for fourteen years.

I was a very mixed-up young woman, looking for external validation, and worrying more about being cute and sexy than being smart and productive. I stepped all over my own career. I strutted around like I was somebody. I gave the impression, "You can't tell me what to do! I have a Master's and you only have a high school diploma!" Who would want to promote that. I carried all my personal drama to work and talked about it incessantly with my co-workers, which led to my first removal (a nice way of saying 'firing'). It didn't help that I did not have a mentor, or a strong first-line supervisor, but a couple of supervisors did try to get the message through to me, e.g. I was fired.

At Strategic Air Command at Offutt Air Base, a major moved me out of my job as an administrative assistant and sent me over to the printing plant, where all I did was receive printing orders. Well, I managed to learn a little from that embarrassment, taking a little bit more professionalism when I was selected to move to the Junior Reserve Officers Training Corps (JROTC) as the Non-Commissioned Officer in Charge (NCOIC). My career recovered a little there. I was even selected for the Deserving Airman's Commissioning Program at the University of Nebraska at Omaha (UNO). I was scheduled to start ROTC classes in the fall, 1980. Once again, pregnancy would keep me from attending college full time.

So instead of going to college, I asked for, and received, a pregnancy discharge in December of that year. Eight months later, I'd moved to Arizona and given birth to a beautiful baby girl. But, I missed working and serving my country. My uniforms were still hanging in my closet. I mentioned this to a friend, and she suggested, "You ought to join the Guard." "What's a Guard?" I asked.

The National Guard is the reserve component of the U.S. military. Its function is to serve as a strategic reserve of the active duty Army and Air Force. Members of the National Guard have been affectionately called 'Weekend Warriors' because they attend military training one weekend a month. Members of the Guard also attend an additional two weeks of training each year. It sounded perfect! I joined the Air National Guard, serving in both Phoenix and Tucson.

Once I finished my bachelor's degree, I went into the Army National Guard Officer Candidate School (OCS). It was a year-long program where you spent two weeks in residence at the beginning and the end, and one weekend each month in between. About six months in, I realized that there was no way I could do the physical fitness part of the training. I called Beau at 1:00 a.m. to come and pick me up. I slunk out, my tail between my legs, and left only a letter of resignation.

For three months I could not look myself in the eye, I was so ashamed of what I had done. I had not had the personal courage or moral fortitude to go in and respectfully admit to the drill instructors that I could not do the training. I went on inactive status for the next five-and-a-half years.

During that inactive military time, I earned my Master's degree in Organizational Communication from ASU and started teaching. My father died. I also finalized my third divorce. And I began intensive personal therapy. It took 18 months to salvage my life.

When Desert Storm kicked off in the summer of 1990, I was ready to serve again. I was willing even if it meant just getting to answer the phone, if only I could wear a uniform again. So I decided to join the Navy Reserve, just to try something different. I had taken all the tests, passed the physical exam, and was just about to sign the papers when a woman in a white uniform walked by.

"Will I have to wear that uniform?" I asked, inclining my head toward the lady in white. "Yes," replied the recruiter. I politely asked for all my paperwork, and I nearly ran out of there. There was no way I could wear white! I'm a klutz—I would have looked like a mess all the time! So I went over to Luke Air Force Base and joined the Air Force Reserve there.

Going back to Luke was coming full circle for me. I was introduced to Luke Air Force Base when I spent the night there with junior high and high school friends. My appreciation for what the world could offer had first been nurtured there. Now I was back as a member of the 944th Fighter Wing, Air Force Reserve unit.

I was 37-years-old, and had been a Staff Sergeant (SSgt) since 1977. I wanted to be promoted, so I went down to the Career Enhancement Program office and asked, "How can I be promoted to Tech Sergeant (TSgt)?" The woman in charge there showed me a little chart: the promotion was dependent upon time in service, time in grade, professional military education (PME), skill level, and a TSgt position vacancy.

I had the time in service and the time in grade requirements nailed. I had the PME and the minimum skill level, but I didn't know of a position vacancy. I was a Staff Sergeant in a SSgt-authorized position. I worked for the Wing Commander as his administrative assistant on drill weekends. But I had impressed my boss, so he submitted my name for the Promotion Enhancement Program, where you can be promoted one grade above the authorized rank for your position. I was finally promoted! Once promoted to TSgt, I was assigned as the NCOIC, Wing Orderly Room.

It was 1992. I had finally learned to take responsibility for my own career. More importantly, I had learned to take responsibility for my own actions. I stayed focused and became results-oriented and a problem solver. I didn't try to look cute.

I had learned the meaning of visible competence. I quit hiding my light under the proverbial bushel. I made sure people were aware of my skills, knowledge, abilities, and experience. I made sure others were aware that I was capable of doing more, and I volunteered to do special projects.

The Wing Commander had a special file folder, labeled "THTD"— Too Hard to Do. He pulled it out and told me I could work on any project in that folder. Within the next couple of years, I finished every project in it. I moved on to work in the Wing Training Office, where I was promoted to Master Sergeant (MSgt) in minimum time.

In my civilian work, I was an organizational development consultant specializing in Total Quality Management. Every Wing in the Air Force had been awarded a Chief Master Sergeant (CMSgt) slot for the Quality Advisor, so I applied for the position. It was a marriage made in heaven for me. I was promoted to Senior Master Sergeant (SMSgt), and worked diligently in the Quality Office, waiting for the minimum time in grade to move up to Chief. By 1996, I was being groomed to go in to the Command Chief's position, which was the highest ranking enlisted position in the organization.

Then my son died, in October, 1996. Two weeks later, I went back to work. My job was to guide the Wing through the preparations for the first Quality Air Force Assessment (QAFA, pronounced café). Although still numb from Alex's death, I focused on the results we needed to achieve. We received an "Excellent" rating on 3 Dec 1996.

At the end of the out-brief from the inspectors, the Medical Group commander came up to me and stated, "You ought to be an officer." I replied, "Sir, I just want to be a Chief." "You ought to be an officer," he repeated. "Sir, I'm too old," I answered. "Not for Medical, you're not." "Sir, I can't stand the sight of blood." He smiled slightly. "It's an Administrative Officer position."

I was surprised. I thought every officer in the Medical Group had to be a doctor or a nurse. "Can I wait and pin on Chief for just one day?" I asked. "When would that be?" he asked. "I just need time in grade. One more year," I answered eagerly. He shook his head. "I can't hold the position open that long. We have a big inspection in eight months and I need help now."

So I asked if I could go home and discuss it with my husband. Dave was a retired Lt. Colonel by then, and if anybody could give me good advice, he could. Dave asked me one defining question, "How much longer do you want to play?" I pondered his question. I was 42 years old, and I felt I had a good five to ten years left in me to serve. However, if I stayed to make Chief, I would be forced to retire in four more years.

You have to be an officer for ten years to retire as an officer, but if I remained for five more years, I would still retire as a SMSgt, which was a respectable retirement rank. I decided to go back to the Colonel and tell him I'd take the job. We put in the paperwork; it took six months to process. I missed Chief by six months.

What I didn't know, however, was that the Commander was working hard to get me commissioned as a Captain instead of a Lieutenant. On the day my orders came in, the Colonel called me up to the front of the room. He read out the commission: "...promoted to the grade of"--he paused dramatically—"CAPTAIN!" I was struck dumb with shock. Everyone cheered, and it was wonderful.

At that point, in May, 1997, I became an officer and began to serve as an Officer in Charge (OIC). I focused on the upcoming inspection and getting the best results. But at that time, I still had not had my "I'm a speck" revelation, nor had I turned my life back over to God. At that time, my life was going great under my own control; who needed God?

Evidently I still needed taking down a notch or two. First, I had the revelation that I was just a speck on the continuum of time. One year later, I acknowledged that maybe I could still make a difference. I finally learned to really let go and let God, when I was diagnosed with cancer.

While recovering from cancer, I had to go inactive from my military career. I needed two doctor's examinations stating I had 'no evidence of disease', at least a year apart, in order to be able to go back to military duty. By March 2002, I was chomping at the bit to go back to work. By then, we had moved to the Washington, D.C. area. I joined the 459th Aeromedical Evacuation Squadron at Andrews Air Force Base, Maryland. I was promoted to Major in 2003, after shepherding my unit through a Health Services Inspection. There is a pattern here: do well on inspections, get promoted.

In 2004, I was deployed to Ramstein Air Base, Germany. The intensive work that is required during wartime is tough, but satisfying. We evacuated 6,200 injured Soldiers, Sailors, Airmen, Marines, and members of the Coast Guard during that tour. We had to work 12-hour days, six days a week. Watching those very young, very badly hurt people coming off those planes was especially hard for me. I kept thinking of Alex, and I ached for the mothers whose sons and daughters were returning to them, broken; alive but broken.

In November 2006, I returned to the ophthalmologist a week after having Lasik eye surgery. I chatted to the doctor about how I was relieved that the Reserves had finally let us undergo this kind of surgery. What I didn't realize was that the doctor was in the Air National Guard. He turned to me quickly. "Reserves? What's your AFSC (Air Force Specialty Code; i.e. occupation)? He then began to grill me about my experience. "Have you had any HSI (Health Services Inspection) experience?" Yeah," I answered, "four times in the last eight years." You'd think I'd handed him a bag of gold coins.

"When can you start?" he said. I was happy in my current position, which had the potential for promotion to Lieutenant Colonel with the potential to be the next Commander. I didn't need to move.

The next day, the Commander of the eye doctor's Medical Group of the DC Air National Guard called me. He also asked, "When can you start?" "Colonel Shea, I'm not looking for a job, but I will come over and help you," I responded.

Two weeks later I met with him, and then conducted a staff assistance visit (like an informal inspection) in January, 2007. Because they are together only once a month, the unit had, in essence, only twenty days to prepare for their inspection in December, 2007. They REALLY needed my help. So I transferred to the 113th Medical Group in the Air National Guard unit; I was promoted to Lt. Colonel in September, 2008, assumed command in October, 2010, and was promoted to Colonel in 2011. I served another 17 years after making the decision to accept my commission in May 1997.

Membership in the National Guard and Reserve components of all the military Services (Army, Navy, Marines, Air Force, and Coast Guard) are an awesome way to serve your country while also making progress on a civilian career. While making my way up the ranks of the military, I also moved my way up in my civil service career with the Department of Defense, retiring in 2014 with 23 years' service. Having reached the ripe old age of 60 years, I also retired from the military in January 2015 with 40 years, zero months, and zero days of service.

After four decades of military experience, I have only two regrets: that I wasted the 14 years from 1977 to 1991; and that I did not get to wear Chief Master Sergeant stripes for at least one day.

Chapter 11

Final Thoughts

The most rewarding thing in my career has been the right and privilege to wear my military uniform. The uniform assured me that I served something greater than myself every day, and it was visible evidence that I served the greatest country on earth. I loved that uniform. Wearing it kept me sane during some of the darkest times of my life. The organization it represented gave me an education, and was the vehicle through which I used every ounce of the God-given gifts granted to me. In serving my country, I have executed skills, obtained knowledge, increased my abilities, improved myself, displayed intelligence, developed and exercised good character, and obtained valuable experience.

When you join the Armed Forces, you are signing a blank check to the people of the United States of America. When you sign that check you do not know how much you are going to give in the end, but you are prepared and willing to give everything you've got to give, up to and including your life.

Over the last 240-plus years, many have cashed that check, paid in full.

It does not matter if you were born rich, poor, or middle class; it does not matter if you are disabled or whole and complete. It only matters where you are going. So, my advice to you is to take responsibility for your success and your failures. Own up to them. Acknowledge them; don't slink off in the middle of the night, like I did. Develop personal and professional courage.

Life is short. It is so short! Mom got 38 years. Alex only had 17.

I, frankly, don't know how many years or days I have left.

We have a choice though: to **get up, suit up, and show up,** each and every day to life or to crawl into the fetal position, pull the covers over our head and just give up.

<u>When life throws you sucker punches,</u>
and all you want to do is pull the covers over your head,
and yell, "Go away cruel world!" and then
call in 'sick and tired' --
there's only one thing left to do, ...

Get up!

Suit up!

Show up!

When you do, for that day, you can claim

VICTORY and SUCCESS!

Each day that you crawl out of bed and
face life with personal courage
makes you stronger.

Chapter 12

The Transition

(added June 2016)

I would like to say that the transition to a civilian retirement went smoothly and without any hitches or qualms. Not true. I spent a year and a half in mourning for my lost identity as a military member. On the morning of June 4th, 2016, I was praying, "Dear Lord, help me understand what I am supposed to do now, and why I can't let go of the military image."

Here is the answer that came to me as I drove to church. My uniform revealed my 40-year history at a glance. When wearing my 'blues' another military person could tell my position, achievements, and career progression. My rank and command pin immediately established my authority. The ribbons on my chest established a 'job well done' and deployments served. The three occupational badges relayed that I had served in nuclear weapons (Missileman Badge), been certified as an Admin troop, and commissioned as a Medical Service Corps (MSC) officer.

This 'at a glance' resume made it possible for me to act from a position of experience, authority, and leadership in a military environment without ever having to relate my history or background. When transferring to a new position or new base, I didn't have to prove myself before making suggestions for improvement, demanding a certain level of performance, or for assigning tasks. When I walked in the door, I was somebody. When I walked through an airport, civilians acknowledged me as someone who serves her country.

When I took off the uniform for the last time on 4 January 2015, all that went away in a single moment. I was back to ground zero. I was one of the masses in an airport or grocery store. I had no purpose or mission. It was the most horrible feeling in my life, second only to my son's death. Not even cancer made me feel so vulnerable. It was worse than being 16-years old and starting from the beginning again, because I knew what success felt and looked like.

My hope back in January of 2015 was that I would move right into being a big mucky-muck consultant, making the big bucks, while wearing business suits, and carrying a briefcase, the civilian symbols of success and importance. That hasn't happened. I have had a few consulting jobs but not continuous with too much time in between jobs. Too much time to think and mourn what I lost.

I now have settled into the volunteer world. I serve on two Home Owners Association (HOA) committees, am President of the local Air Force Association chapter, and volunteer to help in the Kids Ministry at my church. I now realize that my skills, knowledge, and abilities are still the same and can be applied and appreciated in a different environment.

Another recent revelation was that I had equated money to reward and recognition. The volunteer work did not seem as important to me at first. After a year and a half, and working with wonderful volunteers, I realize our country would not be as great without millions of volunteers who want to 'serve' too. While I had served "for my country" for over four decades, these people serve "in" their country every day without pay and with very little recognition.

There are no volunteer ribbons to be worn on their chest. There are no ranks to be admired. They just serve, willingly.

And so, my mournful heart is easing more each day, and my longing for days gone by is slowly fading away.

Here's my advice. Have a transition plan for at least two years before and after the retirement ceremony. This is especially true if you spent more than 30 years in the military or at a single civilian company. I once read that the life expectancy for someone who affiliated with just one organization – military or civilian – for greater than 30 years is just seven years. That thought terrifies me.

It's time to transition to the next great adventure of my life. I have a new grandson to love and spoil, in addition to my five granddaughters. As I held my grandson today, I wondered what Alex would think of his new nephew. Aw, that would have been wonderful, to see Alex embrace this child.

Basically, it is time to practice what I preach: **Get up, suit up, and show up** each and every day to face whatever is coming!

I'm in!

The following are the leadership truisms and lessons learned I have amassed over four decades and are my gift to you.

Penson'isms

Leadership Truisms

of

Paula Francies Penson

President, Francies West, LLC

Colonel, US Air Force, Retired

This booklet is dedicated to ...

My Wing Man,
My battle buddy,
My friend!

Colonel Robert "Darin" Bowie,

113th Wing, Vice Commander, DC Air National Guard

Truism: A statement that is obviously true or that is presented as true.

© December, 2014, Paula Francies Penson, President, Francies West, LLC; © Second edition, January, 2016

The sayings in this book are the figments of imagination and the lessons learned of Colonel Paula F. Penson (retired) based on 42 years in leadership roles across the diverse work-worlds of the service industry, manufacturing, education, university-level academics, civil service, city and federal government, the United States Southern Command, Departments of the Army, Air Force, Navy, the National Guard Bureau, the Army and Air National Guard, and the Air Force Reserve. Any use of them in a military environment is highly encouraged and does not require permission. All others please contact the author for permission at: francieswest@consultant.com

If they could have, they already would have!

People want to be successful every day;

... therefore, if they could have been,

they already would have been successful.

If they could have done the job, it would already be done.

If they could have been successful doing whatever you have asked of them, they would have done it.
If they are not doing what you asked,

then something is missing!

*Your job as a leader is **to find out**!*

So ... what's missing? Is it:

- ☐ *training, education,*
- ☐ *knowledge, understanding,*
- ☐ *motivation, willingness,*
- ☐ *job fit, organization fit,*
- ☐ *capability, ability*
- ☐ *computer systems,*
- ☐ *fear of change,*
- ☐ *fear of failure,*
- ☐ *fear of success,*
- ☐ *fear of embarrassment,*
- ☐ *lack of leadership?*

You own this!

Do not abdicate leadership!

OUTSTANDING ATTRACTS OUTSTANDING!

OUTSTANDING ATTRACTS OUTSTANDING!

When you build an amazing team of just the right people, they will build you an amazing organization.

When they build an amazing organization, it will attract even more amazing people.

Before you know it, you will build an OUTSTANDING team

of people and an OUTSTANDING organization

composed of ordinary people accomplishing

EXTRAORDINARY goals and visions!

First, you have to clean house of the

non-performers before you can start building an

outstanding team. Every subsequent personnel

decision you make is critical! Choose carefully!

Pick and choose the best and the brightest!

Choose only the best fit for your organization.

They match your vision, values, goals, and work ethic.

GOOD PEOPLE WILL LEAVE, BECAUSE THEY CAN!

Good people will leave ... because they can!

Good organizations are looking for good people!

When you "rescue" sub-performers, you **will** lose good performers!

Good people realize that no matter how hard they
work, they are treated the same as the people
who do just enough to get by; or worse,
they are treated the same as incompetent people.

Why should they stay? Why should they work so hard?

People leave supervisors, not organizations.

You cannot build an outstanding organization,
if you rescue and keep sub-performers on the payroll.
For every one you rescue, that's a
position that cannot be used to
hire SHIPS!

There are hundreds of organizations just waiting
to steal your good people!

Those organizations understand the value of rewarding,
recognizing and differentiating the good people.

Surface the
SHIPS!

"Superstars Hiding in Plain Sight!"

Calling all SHIPS!

There are so many "superstars hiding in plain sight" in organizations. These are eager, talented and educated members who are hiding throughout your organization. They are being over-looked and will become demotivated if not "found" and given opportunities to shine!

If you are a true leader, you will actively look for them, identify them, and put them on a fast track for professional development, leadership roles, expanded responsibilities, and developmental experiences. Give them special projects to handle; test them out and let them prove themselves.

Help them set sail!

Got a problem?

Let's
SOLVE IT!©

Give people the tools to solve problems!

To build an outstanding organization, institute a systematic approach to problem solving and reward success.

S –**S**tate the problem

O –**O**rganize efforts

L – **L**ist root causes

V –**V**erify solutions

E –**E**xecute!

I – **I**nstitutionalize results

T –**T**rain Employees

Get
in the
K+A=R!

It's simple math really ...

K – If you have KNOWLEDGE (know your job!)

A – and, you hold yourself and others ACCOUNTABLE,

R – You <u>will</u> achieve RESULTS!

To make this work, however, everyone has to know your vision!

What results are you attempting to achieve?

Make sure everyone knows them!

Knowledge
+ <u>Accountability</u>
= Results

THE FIRST LINE SUPERVISOR IS THE SINGLE-MOST

POWERFUL, IMPACTFUL, INFLUENTIAL

PERSON IN THE ORGANIZATION

FIRST LINE SUPERVISORS

The first line supervisor looks the employee in the eye every day. They know the employees' habits, schedules, work ethic, families, children, finances, and everything that goes into making that employee tick!

If the first line supervisor does not know your leadership vision, you will NOT get there. They are the ones who will be the messenger of your vision, values, and standards, and ensure your employees get on board and make it happen.

Invest in your first line supervisors!

Give them training, education, and knowledge.

Ensure the first line supervisor understands that their role is to:

Train 'em

Trust 'em

Get out of the way

Pick up the pieces

Pat 'em on the back!

The five phases of supervision:

1. Training = mentorship phase
2. Trusting = leadership phase
3. Getting out of the way = empowerment phase
4. Picking up pieces = feedback/improvement
5. Patting on the back = recognition phase

Three Guiding Principles of Leadership

1. Back to basics
2. Never walk past a mistake
3. Each one, teach one

Reset back to basics!

Sometimes you have to rebuild your organization

from the ground up.

1. Get back to basics!
a. Ensure everyone knows the job.
b. Ensure they know where they fit into the overall vision.

2. Never walk past a mistake!
a. Every time you walk past a mistake, you condone that behavior and it will become embedded into your culture.
b. Get back on track and ensure everyone knows the job standards, ethical boundaries, and the expectations for civil behavior.

3. Each one, teach one!
a. Let people teach each other.
b. The best way to learn anything is to have to teach it.
c. Send people to training, then make them trainers.

Develop people through the ...

BASICS©
of
Feedback

These are the steps for administering effective feedback.

BEHAVIOR

Reflect back to them their exact behavior; do not editorialize or soften.

ATTITUDE

Describe their attitude about their behavior.
"You don't appear to care that you were late to work."

STANDARDS

Relate the company policy that forbids their behavior; quote the company policy manual, law, or regulation.

IMPACT

Tell them how their behavior affected the organization or co-workers.

CONSEQUENCES

Identify the consequences for their behavior.

SOLUTIONS

The employee owns the solution(s) to the problem.
Have the employee define how to keep the behavior from happening again in an improvement plan: <u>Employee will do what by when.</u>

Take the time to

BE STILL!

At the beginning of every day!

B²E STIL³L³!

At some point in your lifetime, you will realize that success is NOT measured by fancy cars, big houses, or material things! Success is measured by how much you impact others' lives. I encourage you to **B²E STIL³L³** each and every day, and you will know true success!

BE BRAVE EVERY day! Face the tough challenges of life and do the right thing, even when it is not the popular thing.

SERVE something greater than yourself each day.

TEACH everything you can possibly teach.

INSPIRE others to achieve their fullest potential.

LEARN³ everything you're supposed to learn, each and every day. First, LEARN about yourself, for you are still a work in progress. Second, LEARN about the needs of others, and help where you can. Third, LEARN about the subjects on which you're supposed to be the subject matter expert and be a good steward to your employer.

LISTEN twice as much as you talk, for you can't learn anything new if you're doing all the talking!

LOVE unconditionally and generously, no matter race, color, religion, gender, age, height, weights, size, shape, or any other demographic we insist upon labeling each other.

LEAD, from wherever you sit!

America needs leadership more than we've ever needed it before! Whether you are a supervisor, manager, parent, teacher, employer, student, military member, for America's sake, please **LEAD!**

Colonel Penson's Personal Cornerstones of Success

1. VISIBLE COMPETENCE
a. Bottom line up front: Know your job!
b. Other people must see it.

2. HUMBLE CONFIDENCE
a. Have confidence.
b. Not cockiness.

3. PERSONAL ACCOUNTABILITY
a. Fulfill your requirements.
b. Don't ever have to be told to meet your obligations!

4. PERSONAL COURAGE
a. Do the right thing!
b. Even when your boss is wrong.
c. Even when it means you might lose your job.

5. SELFLESS SERVICE
a. Serve something greater than yourself every day!
b. Don't be self-serving! You are not fooling anyone.

6. POSITIONAL LEADERSHIP
a. Lead from wherever you sit!
b. Make suggestions for improvement.

7. UNDAUNTED PERSEVERANCE
a. Never give up! If at first you don't succeed, …
b. Look in the mirror first; are you the problem?

8. GET UP, SUIT UP, AND SHOW UP EVERY DAY!
a. When life throws you **sucker punches**, there is only one thing left to do: get up, suit up, and show up every day! Then you can claim **VICTORY** over life!
b. If you serve, teach, inspire, learn, listen, and love every day, then your life is a **SUCCESS.** And if you also get to _lead_, then your life is truly **BLESSED!**

BIOGRAPHY

COLONEL (RET) PAULA F. PENSON

Colonel (Ret) Paula Francies Penson has resumed her position as President, *Francies West, LLC*, an organizational and leadership development corporation, after serving in support of the on-going Global War on Terrorism since 9/11/2001. Her business organization consults on: Leadership Training and Development, Team Building, MBTI administration, Program Management, Process and Quality Control, Problem Solving, BASICS of Feedback, and conducts Organizational and Climate Assessments. Francies West was incorporated in 1997.

Col Penson retired after 40 years of service on 4 Jan 2015. She previously served as Special Assistance for Leadership Development and AFSO21 for the 113th Wing, DC Air National Guard from Jan 2014 to Jan 2015. She commanded the 113th Medical Group from Oct 2010 to Jan 2014. Prior to assuming command, she was the full-time Senior Administrator/Medical Administrative Officer, 113th Medical Group since Feb 2008.

Col Penson's civilian career paralleled her military assignments with civil service positions in the Department of the Navy, the Army National Guard (National Guard Bureau) and Congressional Affairs for U.S. Southern Command (SOUTHCOM) (joint assignment). Her civilian career experience includes Faculty Associate, Arizona State University; Faculty, Maricopa County Community Colleges; Organizational Development (OD) Manager for McDonnell Douglas Helicopter Company; First Line Supervisor, Ozarka Water Company and OD Consultant to Perrier Group of America, and President of her own consulting company, Francies West, LLC.

EDUCATION

Pursuing, EdD, Organizational Leadership; Grand Canyon University, AZ
1987 M.A. Organizational Communication, Arizona State, Tempe, Arizona
1983 B.S. Communication, Arizona State University, Tempe, Arizona
1983 AAS, Administration, CCAF, Maxwell AFB, Alabama

AWARDS & DECORATIONS

Legion of Merit; Meritorious Service Medal (4); AF Commendation Medal (2); Army Commendation Medal; AF Achievement Medal; Army Achievement Medal; AF Outstanding Unit Award (5); Army Superior Unit Award; National Defense Service Medal (3); Global War on Terrorism

---

For Motivational Speaking

or training classes

Contact **Francies West, LLC** at:

francieswest@consultant.com

➤ **BASICS**© of Feedback Training Sessions

➤ Climate Surveys and Customized Debriefings

➤ Continuous Process Improvement training and team facilitation

➤ Customer Service Climate Surveys

➤ Executive and Senior Leader Training

➤ First Line Supervisor Training: **Surface the SHIPS!**

➤ Leadership Training and Development

➤ Middle Management Leadership Training

➤ Motivational Speaking Engagements: **BE STILL!**

➤ Myers Briggs Type Indicator (MBTI) certified administrator and trainer

➤ Problem Solving Model Training **(SOLVE IT!**©**)** & Train-the-Trainer

➤ Program Management 101 Training and Development

➤ Process and Quality Control Assessment

➤ Organizational Assessments

➤ Organizational Culture Assessments

➤ Team Building Exercises and Facilitation

➤ Train-the-Trainer Customized Development

The net proceeds of this book are donated to the Alex Francies college scholarship fund for military members and dependents.

This book includes:

> **When life throws you sucker punches,**
>
> there's only one thing left to do:
>
> **GET UP, SUIT UP, and SHOW UP**
>
> Each and every day to life!
>
> - Raised in poverty as a migrant worker
> - Teenage pregnancy at 17
> - Gave up child for adoption at 18
> - Father shot and killed mother at age 18
> - Attempted suicide at 22
> - Divorced three times by the age of 35
> - Fired three times by the age of 35
> - Killed a person in car accident at age 40
> - 17-year old son died at age 42
> - Diagnosed with cancer at age 47

Penson'isms

10 Leadership truisms

Lessons learned from 40+ years of experience and leadership positions became truisms. These hard-won lessons were proven repeatedly in real-world work environments including manufacturing, education, academia, civil service, the service industry, as a government contractor, and in all branches of the United States military.

Made in the USA
Middletown, DE
27 August 2019